PARADIPLOMACY

GLOBAL PRACTICES AND LESSONS LEARNT

ABSTRACT

The subnational governments (state governments) have become the potential actors in international politics; this phenomenon is called 'paradiplomacy'. The term 'paradiplomacy' is an abbreviation of 'parallel diplomacy', which means that states and their subnational governments oversee foreign engagements to further their interests in the international arena.[1] The increasing integration of the economy and interdependence on trade in the early 1980s caused subnational governments and entities to practice paradiplomacy. Even though the conduct of national diplomacy remains the exclusive domain of sovereign states or the union government as principal actors, state governments play a supplementary role, especially in the federal countries. The federal countries have decentralised the conduct of their foreign policies, providing scope for their subnational units to get involved in diplomatic affairs as actors.

India is a classic example that has resorted to paradiplomacy, of late, probably to expedite its economic prowess and political clout in the world. As India has integrated with the globalisation process and registered the fastest economic growth while promoting the state governments to play a big role in external engagements, can it be argued that paradiplomacy in India is an off-shoot of these two processes? This book attempts to analyse the role of Indian states and cities as emerging paradiplomatic actors who have been engaged in many economic and cultural programmes in collaboration with foreign subnational governments. Given India's current extensive engagement with the world and growing foreign interactions of Indian state governments, the practice of paradiplomacy seems to be an integral and evolving approach in the country's foreign policy discourse. The book attempts to study paradiplomacy as a concept and its growing practice in international relations, followed by an in-depth analysis of India's paradiplomatic endeavours during the last few decades. The study attempts to theorise paradiplomacy as an emerging field of inquiry in the academic discourse, followed by an extensive analysis of India's paradiplomatic endeavours in its foreign policy.

Note

1. Rodrigo Tavares, *Paradiplomacy: Cities and States as Global Players* (New York: Oxford University Press, 2016).

PARADIPLOMACY

GLOBAL PRACTICES AND LESSONS LEARNT

DEVANSHI SHAH

KW Publishers Pvt Ltd
New Delhi

ISBN 978-81-978433-9-6 Paperback

Published in India by Kalpana Shukla

KW Publishers Pvt Ltd
4676/21, First Floor, Ansari Road
Daryaganj, New Delhi 110 002
Phone: +91 11 43528107
Marketing: kw@kwpub.in
Editorial: production@kwpub.in
Website: www.kwpub.in

Printed and bound in India

Contents

Foreword

The evolution of diplomacy as a foreign policy tool has a chequered history. Often modern diplomacy is viewed to have begun with the Peace of Westphalia in 1648, which is studied concerning national sovereignty and central authority's prerogatives with other actors. But in Indic knowledge having more than three thousand five hundred years of history, diplomacy or *Rājanaya* is much more than the diplomacy of states and governments. *Rājanaya* is composed of the terms rājan and nāya which involves rājanīti, nīti, and rājavidyā or politics, policy, and statesmanship. Kautilya's Arthsashastra, an ancient Indian Sanskrit treatise on statecraft, political science, economic policy, military strategy, and much more, aptly reveals how dynamic and diverse diplomacy could be. However, the latest evolutionary strand is the decentralization of diplomatic actors and activities in the diplomatic arena, in other words known as the 'paradiplomacy'. This book is an inexorable attempt by Dr. Devanshi to fathom the latest strand in the evolution of diplomacy and inquiry into best practices followed by other actors that India can espouse.

At the outset, the book scrutinizes the theoretical narratives of paradiplomacy during the 1960s when diplomacy started to be perceived as not state-centric. Subsequently, during the 1990s scholars and practitioners explored the concept intensively and coined numerous terminologies but owing to contextual variance, the discourse is yet to be counted as an independent academic discipline within modern diplomatic studies. This study elaborates on the interconnected practical forms of paradiplomacy and examines how subnational governments (state governments) have formed paradiplomatic engagements through multifarious domains. It brings to the fore the four stages of paradiplomacy practice.

Though the phrase Paradiplomacy was not in usage, the practice of such activity can be linked to the ancient 'city diplomacy' that gave importance to trade, commerce, and cultural linkages. The city-states of Mohenjo-Daro and Harappa in South Asia were the urban centres known for their extensive trade links in the Indus region. The author has delved into ancient history to understand the city engagements; the city networks of the Mesopotamian civilizations, the trade links of Mesoamerican civilizations, the ancient Silk Road during the Han dynasty, the extensive road networks in the Western Roman Empire, the European cities urbanizing in the 16th century, and the growth of urban cities in the 20th century, etc. were in fact paradiplomacy of those eras.

In modern times, paradiplomacy was practiced mostly in Western federal countries, such as Canada, Germany, Belgium, Switzerland, the US (Australia in the East), and some unitary countries like Spain and France. Later in the 21st century, it became a noteworthy practice in countries like Argentina, Brazil, Chile, China, India, Japan, Mexico, Russia and South Africa. Gradually the most common form of paradiplomatic engagements became the sister-city and town-twinning agreements based on specific issues such as common economic growth and environmental protection. This way, the concept of paradiplomacy does not challenge the traditional notion of diplomacy; rather, it broadens the scope of diplomatic actions and can be viewed as supplementary diplomacy or furtherance of national diplomacy. But the term 'parallel diplomacy', the abbreviation of paradiplomacy, does not explicitly express it so.

In the contemporary world, the increasing activism of megacities in addressing urgent global agendas such as environmental challenges, dealing with health emergencies, disaster mitigation, trade facilitation, etc. have changed the ceremonial notion of paradiplomatic practices. When the central/union government is under tremendous pressure from mounting political tensions, the subsidiary governments/state governments have to take up the responsibility to negotiate on behalf of the entire nation or province concerned, thereby assuming centre stage; a bright example is the role of cities in global climate change negotiations.

India is not an onlooker in the era of paradiplomacy. Indian states and cities are off-late getting involved in foreign policy conduct. Post-independence, for the growing pressure of state-building and nation-building process, cities and states played minimal roles. Only after the economic reform adopted during 1990s, provincial governments and megacities were encouraged to carry forward the LPG agenda to boost FDI inflow, economic growth, and infrastructure development. One can therefore argue that India's paradiplomacy was more of an economic compulsion than a diplomatic offshoot. Therefore, India has yet to develop a concrete paradiplomatic policy framework to bring a level playing field for all actors though many state governments and cities have become paradiplomatic actors during the last three decades.

As the author rightly asserts, the paradiplomatic practice in India is marred with several limitations, one such being the lack of consensus between the Union and the States. Furthermore, paradiplomacy is not fully incorporated within India's foreign policy as most of the sister city tie-ups are still at a preliminary stage. However, India will not roll back its paradiplomatic initiatives, therefore, adopting best practices from countries like China and Brazil, that have extensively used paradiplomacy as a foreign policy tool, would be prudent. In the neighborhood, China's 'Urban Diplomacy' has helped it to enhance its cross-border interaction and regional cooperation. The paradiplomatic attempts set out by China have strengthened its cities' international influence. Chinese experience can be of much help to India. Similarly, the 'Municipal Foreign Policy' of Brazil sets an example to institutionalize paradiplomacy with a proper mandate. The paradiplomatic structures established at a local level have encouraged the keen involvement of Brazilian mayors and local authorities in addressing urban issues. India can extrapolate them. As India is a newcomer in this domain, the imperative is to devise a robust mechanism and policy framework to integrate Indian states and cities in foreign policy conduct. A municipalization or decentralization of Indian diplomatic efforts is warranted as India is aspiring to join the big leagues by achieving exponential economic growth and geopolitical weightage.

It is in this context that Dr Devanshi Shah has produced her commendable study giving us a peep into the outgrowth of diplomacy in general and Indian diplomatic excellence in particular. She has gone through all possible information on the domain and has put together an objective study that provides the foundations to understand Indian diplomatic personality, nomenclature, and future trajectory. The volume is a must for anyone and everyone interested in Indian diplomacy and geopolitics.

Dr. **Sitakanta Mishra**
Dean, School of Liberal Studies
Pandit Deendayal Energy University, Gujarat, India

Acknowledgements

The completion of this book took immense effort, time, and dedication. At each step of this book, there was generous support from my mentor Dr. Sitakanta Mishra who motivated me to write this book. I express my gratitude to him for giving me his valuable time and sincere contributions to my research. I dedicate this book to my late father, Nrupesh Shah. He was and remains to be my leading light. I am deeply grateful to my mother, Hina Shah for giving me moral strength in my trying times. I thank my sister, Karishma, and my husband, Neel for their unconditional love and support.

At last, I sincerely thank Ms. Kalpana Shukla and the KW Publisher team for giving me this opportunity to publish with them.

Acknowledgment

Tables and Figures

Tables

Figures

Acronyms

AEI	American Enterprise Institute
AIMF	Association of Francophone Mayors
ARF	Assessoria De Relações Federativas
ASEM	Asia-Europe Meeting
AZRF	Arctic Zone of the Russian Federation
BRI	Belt Road Initiative
CCP	Chinese Communist Party
CEMR	Council of European Municipalities and Regions
CLGF	Commonwealth Local Government Forum
CNM	Confederação Nacional De Municípios
CoR	Committee of Region
CPAFFC	Chinese People's Association for Friendship with Foreign Countries
DPC	Dabhol Power Company
DSCI	Denver Sister Cities International
EECI	Energy Efficient Cities Initiative
EIRA	European Industrial Regions Association
EODB	Ease of Doing Business
FDI	Foreign Direct Investment
FNP	Frente Nacional De Prefeitos
GDP	Gross Domestic Product
GHG	Greenhouse Gas
GMS	Greater Mekong Subregion
ICLEI	Local Governments for Sustainability
IOR-ARC	Indian Ocean Rim Association of Regional Cooperation

ISCS	Inter-State Council Secretariat
IULA	International Union of Local Authorities
MEA	Ministry of External Affairs
MHA	Ministry of Home Affairs
MNC	Multinational Corporation
MOU	Memorandum of Understanding
NAFTA	North American Free Trade Agreement
NASDA	National Association of State Development Agencies
NCG	Non-Central Government
NGO	Non-Governmental Organisation
NPC	National People's Congress
NYC	New York City
OCO	Office of Coordination and Orientation
ORU-FOGAR	Un Region Organization/Forum of Regional Governments and Global Association of Regions
PIOCCI	People of Indian Origin Chamber of Commerce and Industry
SEA	States' External Activities
TAT	Tourism Authority of Thailand
UCLG	United Cities and Local Governments
UK	United Kingdom
UN	United Nations
UNCSD	United Nations Conference on Sustainable Development
UN-DESA	United Nations Department of Economic and Social Affairs
UNDP	United Nations Development Programme
UNFCCC	United Nations Framework Convention on Climate Change
USA	United States of America
UT	Union Territory
WEF	World Economic Forum
WSF	World Social Forum
WTO	World Trade Organization

Glossary

Term	**Definition**
Paradiplomacy	An abbreviation of 'parallel diplomacy' that involves subnational governments like cities and substates who engage with foreign cities and states.
Subnational Government	The sum of state governments, local and regional governments.
Substates	Subdivision of a state, such as cities and towns.
Sister-Cities/Town Twinning	A legal agreement between two geographically and politically distinct cities to promote cultural and economic diplomacy.
City-Diplomacy	An interaction of cities with foreign cities on a global scale.
Protodiplomacy	A political activism where a local government seeks international legitimacy to form its own independent state.
Climate Cities	Climate Cities are dedicated cities who have taken a global outlook towards combating climate change through multilateral networks.
Global Cities	A group of powerful cities that are key urban centres for the global economic system. These cities develop international city networks and conduct their own foreign policy.

Competitive Federalism	A concept where states and UTs compete with each other, which subsequently drives the economic growth of the country.
Cooperative Federalism	A concept of a stable relationship between the centre and state to improve coordination on issues of common interests.
Urban Diplomacy	A concept that includes cooperation among sister-cities through global partnerships, addressing common agendas and increasing economic ties.

1

Introduction

The subnational governments (state governments) have become the potential actors in international politics; this phenomenon is called 'paradiplomacy'. The term 'paradiplomacy' is an abbreviation of 'parallel diplomacy', which means that the states and their subnational governments oversee foreign engagements. The increasing integration of the economy and interdependence on trade in the early 1980s caused subnational governments and entities to practice paradiplomacy. Even though the conduct of national diplomacy remains the exclusive domain of sovereign states or the union government as principal actors, state governments play a supplementary role, especially in the federal countries. The federal countries have decentralised the conduct of their foreign policies, providing scope for their subnational units as actors to get involved in diplomatic affairs. India is a classic example that has resorted to paradiplomacy, of late, probably to expedite its economic prowess and political clout in the world. As India has integrated with the globalisation process and registered the fastest economic growth while promoting state governments to play a big role in external engagements, can it be argued that paradiplomacy in India is an off-shoot of these two processes? This book attempts to analyse the role of Indian states and cities as emerging paradiplomatic actors who have been engaged in many economic and cultural programmes in collaboration with foreign subnational governments. Given India's current extensive engagement with the world and growing foreign interactions of Indian state governments, the practice of paradiplomacy seems to be an integral and evolving approach in its foreign policy discourse. The book attempts to study paradiplomacy as a concept and its growing practice in international relations, followed by an in-depth analysis of India's paradiplomatic endeavours during the last few decades.

The concept of paradiplomacy emerged in the 1970s when western countries, such as the USA and Canada inculcated the theory of paradiplomacy within the study of diplomacy. The liberal democracies integrated local and regional governments with foreign substates (constituent units of a state) in matters like trade, commerce, technology, education, climate change, etc. Later, in the 1990s, some of the European substates such as "Flanders in Belgium, Basque County in Spain and Catalonia had enhanced their economic diplomacy by establishing foreign relations at micro level."[1] The regional provinces, cities and substates became the paradiplomatic actors and eroded the economic and cultural boundaries between the states.[2] Initially, Canada, Germany, Belgium, Switzerland, Australia, Spain, France and USA were the only countries where paradiplomacy was acknowledged as a part of foreign policy.[3] This gained wide acceptance in the 21st century when sub-states of "Argentina, Brazil, Chile, China, India, Japan, Mexico, Russia and South Africa ventured into paradiplomatic activities with foreign countries."[4] The approach towards paradiplomacy has never been homogenous among the countries due to their diverse governance structures. Due to this, paradiplomacy is dynamic in nature and, therefore, its practice varies from country to country. Through paradiplomacy, cities have engaged in global affairs in various domains, such as climate change, economic cooperation, regional integration, sustainable development, etc. Thus, the concept of paradiplomacy, being interdisciplinary in its approach, does not have a uniform definition.

Paradiplomacy gained recognition in India in the 1990s when the country liberalised its economy and integrated it with the global economy. Recently, the practice of paradiplomacy became a prominent subject of foreign policy debate when Prime Minister Narendra Modi called for "greater role for states in India's economic diplomacy."[5] In his inaugural address at the Delhi Economics Conclave in November 2015, Prime Minister Narendra Modi stated that:

> "In a break with over 65 years of tradition, we have involved states even in foreign policy. The Ministry of External Affairs has been asked to work with the states. When I visited China, a state-to-state summit was also

held. And states have been asked to create export promotion councils. Making the states think globally is yet another reform with the potential to transform."[6]

Often, Prime Minister Modi's speeches have clearly indicated that paradiplomacy would be the essential component in the foreign policy of India. Since 2013, the participation of Indian state governments in the dealings with various foreign governments in the domain of investments, sister-city agreements and cultural collaborations has relatively increased. This growing interaction between the state governments and foreign governments compelled the Ministry of External Affairs (MEA) to establish a 'States Division' that could increase cooperation between the union and the states on matters of foreign policy.[7] The MEA has stated that the chief function of this new division is "to facilitate states to expand their external linkages through training and capacity building in areas related to exports, tourism and culture and further attract more overseas investment and expertise."[8] Indian states would play a vital role in expanding commercial and cultural diplomacy.

Since 2015, the central government has placed more emphasis on paradiplomatic activities, but its practice is not yet thorough in its conduct. Most of the twinning and sister-city agreements are concluded by the MEA; the role of the state government is merely confined to facilitating foreign visits and programmes. Although the state governments are consulted by the MEA before the signing of agreements, they have minimal influence in foreign policy matters. In addition, the Indian constitution still lacks the mandate to determine the role of the states in India's foreign policy. Within the Indian constitution, the state governments, as per Article 246, have limited power to conduct external relations. This study suggests putting in place an institutional apparatus to develop a dedicated channel of communication for states to effectively carry out their diplomatic activities.

The growing diplomatic activities between the cities of different nations have made it apparent that paradiplomacy has started gaining wide recognition in Asian countries like China, India and Japan. At the same time, the global trends have indicated that metropolitan cities are the fulcrum of geoeconomics.[9] The World Economic Forum predicts that around 15 cities shall become economic and political powerhouses by 2030.[10] These cities are accelerating their international activism across the globe, which has paved the way for mayors, governors and city leaders to exercise their economic as well as political power in the global agenda. Multilateral networking is one such platform, where delegates from municipal and state governments discuss local governance and issues pertaining to it in a global context. At present, there are 125 multilateral networks and forums of subnational governments that focus on issues ranging from sustainable development to culture, education and urban development. Currently, over 200 intercity networks are working together to tackle issues ranging from migration and pollution to climate change.

In addition, globalisation has penetrated the traditional methods of the states' diplomatic affairs. However, the context of paradiplomacy does not change the fact that the states are the primary unit of analysis, but changes the course of interaction between the states. It is a phenomenon that does not challenge the traditional notion of diplomacy; rather, it broadens the scope of diplomatic studies and its practice in international relations. Paradiplomacy in India is an economic compulsion rather than a diplomatic offshoot. This study also inquires how India should use paradiplomacy as part of its foreign policy, with lessons from China and Brazil, to enhance its global stature in the realm of international diplomacy.

Conceptualizing Paradiplomacy

The concept of paradiplomacy emerged in the academic discourse in the beginning of the 1960s, when diplomacy was no longer perceived as state-centric. The theoretical narrative of paradiplomacy stems from the Liberal school of thought. Neo-liberal thinkers like Robert Keohane and Joseph Nye, who coined the Complex Interdependence theory, have ascertained that "the international corporations have developed transnational relations by conducting coalition and interaction across state boundaries, which are not controlled by central foreign policy organs of government."[11] This phenomenon can be termed as 'transnational relations', which seems to have "faded the distinction between domestic politics and international affairs."[12]

The mid-20th century observed the transnational revolution that created a global trend of bringing new actors in international affairs. The involvement of new actors increased issues such as trade and investments, education and environmental problems in 'low politics' in the global affairs agenda. For example, in Canada, during the 1960s, "the Quiet Revolution in Quebec under the new Liberal government (Jean Lesage)" demanded the involvement of the provinces in international relations.[13] The revolutions were carried out in "Brussels, Chicago, Frankfurt, London, Los Angeles, Milan and Paris, which left a strong impact on paradiplomacy development in Quebec."[14] Further, in the 1970s, the 'new federalism' model was adopted by then US President Richard Nixon.[15] The intent of this model was to delegate "some federal programs and shift funds, authority and responsibility to states and local governments in an effort to more effectively manage the intergovernmental grant system."[16] The low politics issues, which were under the jurisdiction of the local and regional authorities, became a concern for the international community.[17] This further encouraged the subnational governments to play an active role in international politics. For instance, in USA, the National Governors Association established the International Trade and Foreign Relations Committee.[18] Similarly, the National Association of State Development Agencies (NASDA), National League of Cities and US Conference of Mayors were established to signify states and cities as global actors in the international forum.[19] Thus, paradiplomacy emerged as a new phenomenon to mark the rise of subnational governments that were competent enough to act and seek global influence. Apparently, this shift attracted political scientists and scholars to provide a conceptual framework of paradiplomacy and analyse its implications.

The word 'para' is actually derived from a Greek word that means 'near' or 'subsidiary'.[20] Rohan Butler used the term 'paradiplomacy' in 1961 in his collective monograph, "Studies in Diplomatic History and Historiography", under the title 'Paradiplomacy'.[21] He further defines it as a personal and parallel diplomacy that "complements and competes with the regular foreign policy of the concerned ministers."[22] However, the term, under Butler's interpretation,[23] did not gain a favourable reception in the academic community. The term 'parallel diplomacy' did not wholly justify the activities conducted within the notion of paradiplomacy. Later, in the 1980s, the term was revived by Ivo Duchacek and Panayotis Soldatos.[24] Duchacek (1984), in his article, "The International Dimension of Subnational Self-Government", has linked the notion of paradiplomacy to 'transborder regionalism' and 'global microdiplomacy', both of which serve as instruments for subnational governments to conduct interactions outside national boundaries.[25] According to Duchacek, transborder regionalism is not a new concept as it preceded the Westphalian order when subnational transborder interactions played a significant role in the "cross-boundary movements of products, persons and pollutants."[26] In the wake of globalisation, the role of subnational governments was redefined due to their political influence in global issues and the growing complexities within their cross-border interactions. It seems that paradiplomacy is a natural offshoot of globalisation that branched out from the traditional notions of sovereignty, which this book attempts to examine.

The term 'global micro-diplomacy'[27] mainly describes the pattern of subnational governments who seek "cooperation far beyond the immediate neighbours and establish relations in the distant corners of the world."[28] For instance, Alberta has established foreign representatives not only in Houston, Los Angeles, New York, Tokyo and Hong Kong, but has also extended its relationship in the province of Heilongjiang in the People's Republic of China and the province of Gangweon-do in South Korea.[29] Duchacek has associated microdiplomacy as a substitute of paradiplomacy in his monograph, titled *The Territorial Dimension of Politics: Within, Among, Across Nations*. Under this, he provides four distinct, yet interconnected forms of paradiplomacy,[30] which are:

1. **Transborder regional microdiplomacy**—formal and informal interactions predominantly confined to geographic proximity.
2. **Transregional microdiplomacy**—connections at the regional level and the negotiations held between non-central governments (NCG).[31]
3. **Global paradiplomacy**—trade and industrial or cultural activities carried out by non-central governments in other countries as well as their association with different divisions and agencies of foreign governments.
4. **Protodiplomacy**—initiatives and activities undertaken by non-central governments that determine social, economic as well as cultural relations with foreign nations. [32]

In 1985, the Canadian Institute of International Affairs organised a conference titled "The Provinces and Canadian Foreign Policy" to establish paradiplomacy as a field of study in foreign affairs. The conference was attended by officials from the provinces of Alberta, Newfoundland, Saskatchewan, Ontario and Quebec.[33] Such initiatives led to emergence of paradiplomacy as an innovative concept that emphasised the involvement of subnational governments in international relations. But, the research conducted in this field of study was descriptive and merely based on case studies. The terminology lacked a strong discourse and a theoretical framework. This void was later filled by the research scholar, Panayotis Soldatos, who constructed an explanatory framework of paradiplomacy by providing theoretical insights.[34] Soldatos and Duchacek gradually became strong proponents of paradiplomacy in the 1980s. Their explanatory framework was favourably accepted in the academic community as there was hardly any substantial alternative at that time. Soldatos has defined paradiplomacy "as a direct international activity by subnational actors supporting, complementing, correcting, duplicating or challenging the nation-states' diplomacy."[35]

In 1990, the domain of paradiplomacy strengthened as scholars and practitioners started exploring the concept. John Kincaid proposed a new term 'constituent diplomacy' in place of 'paradiplomacy'.[36] According to Kincaid, the prefix 'para' only emphasises the action, but fails to determine the "nature of the actor who promotes these activities."[37] Constituent diplomacy is a relatively advanced approach as it identifies the constituent unit/government as the actor that conducts these diplomatic activities.[38] These constituent governments comprise "states, provinces, cantons, landers, republics, municipalities and even port authorities."[39] John Kincaid used the term to shape the foreign policy for local bodies that is in accordance with the democratic federal structure of the government. For instance, major USA municipalities, such as Dallas, were engaged in foreign relations by developing their own diplomatic protocol officers. In 1982, New York carried out its own trade relations in England followed by West Germany.[40]

One can find that the research in paradiplomacy in the beginning was only confined to American and Canadian scholars. This trend shifted in 1992, when the Maastricht Treaty led to the creation of the European Union and in 1994, paradiplomacy gained a new impetus at a supranational level due to the establishment of the Committee of Region (CoR), an organisation within the EU.[41] The CoR provided opportunities to the subnational entities of European countries, such as Flanders (Belgium), Catalonia and Basque (Spain) along with other regions with "political, cultural, economic and linguistic aspirations to represent themselves as international actors."[42] The INTREG programme was another EU initiative to assist economic and strategic cross-border cooperation among subnational governments.[43]

So far, innumerable discussions have emerged on the usage of the terms in the present context of paradiplomacy. Authors such as Michael Keating and Francisco Aldecoa have referred to the term 'subnational government/ actors' as "public authorities at a regional level below sovereign state." Terms such as 'region', 'regional governments', 'constituent government/unit' and 'subnational government/actor' are acknowledged as "synonymic and are used in an interchangeable manner."[44]

The term 'paradiplomacy' was gradually challenged by scholars, which led to the emergence of new terms in correlation with the existing ones. For instance, Brian Hocking proposed the term 'multi-layered diplomacy' to describe the densely interconnected web in which non-central governments "are capable of performing a variety of goals at different points in the negotiating process. In so doing, they may become opponents of national objectives, but, equally, they can serve as allies and agents in pursuit of those objectives."[45] Charlie Jeffery introduced the term 'trans-federal' relations that emphasised transborder actions and interactions developing in the region. 'Federative diplomacy' was another term popularised in Brazil in the 1990s by then Minister of External Relations Luiz Felipe Lampreia.[46]

The Fourth Lomé Convention of 1989 introduced 'Decentralised International Cooperation' to vindicate a cooperation and partnership between the EU and the African, Caribbean and Pacific countries. Later, in 2008, the United Nations Development Programme (UNDP) used this term to determine the direct relationship between regional territories based on the partnership between communities in different cities and towns. The term is often used by the Euro-African Partnership for Decentralised Governance, supported by the United Nations Development of Economic and Social Affairs (UN-DESA).[47]

Various scholars have provided relevant criticisms to the usage of the term 'paradiplomacy'. Hocking has contended that the word 'diplomacy' is a traditional phenomenon of international politics.[48] With the usage of this term, diplomacy has assumed a domestic dimension among NCGs; therefore, under this pretext, the concept of 'diplomacy' itself needs a new definition to understand the true essence of paradiplomacy.[49] Another scholar, Iňaki

Aguirre, has stated that paradiplomacy has emerged as a post-modernist discourse to provide a theoretical insight on the contemporary forms of diplomacy. Aguirre has pointed out that the concept has failed to inquire about the evolving nature and contemporary meaning of NCG's involvement in the international arena.[50]

Ever since, the term 'paradiplomacy' is widely used among policymakers and scholars. Besides paradiplomacy, there are different terms that conceptualise the regional pursuits in the international domain, such as 'constituent diplomacy', 'regional diplomacy', 'sub-state diplomacy', 'subnational foreign policy', 'local government external action', 'local diplomacy', 'local foreign policy', 'regional diplomacy', 'microdiplomacy', 'plurinational diplomacy', multi-layered diplomacy', 'catalytic diplomacy', 'protodiplomacy' and 'post- diplomacy'. All of the above-stated terminologies do not have a clear definition and therefore, these neologisms[51] can easily deviate from their meaning when used in different contexts.[52] Alexander Kuznetsov has, thus, provided an apt definition of paradiplomacy as "a form of political communication for reaching economic, cultural and political or any other types of benefits, the core of which consists in the self-sustained actions of regional governments with foreign governmental and non-governmental actors."[53]

Multi-dimensional Scope of Paradiplomacy

Given the variety of terminologies of paradiplomacy and their contextual variance, the scope of paradiplomacy as an activity is very wide and includes multifarious domains. According to Kuznetsov, there are mainly 11 domains where subnational governments could engage in paradiplomacy:

1. **Constitutional:** As suggested by Samuel Huntington, 'transnational revolution' has effaced the distinction that exists between the 'high politics' and 'low politics' due to the involvement of new actors.[54] This is elaborated in Nye's concept of 'soft power' as the key to "global governance that has ultimately prioritized educational policies in the international agenda."[55] In the book *Federal Constitutions and International Relations,* John Trone has discussed that the subnational governments are involved in external relations through "two aspects: (1) what level of legal permission of making treaty with foreign actors is granted by the national constitutions

to regional authorities and (2) the constitutional requirements for consultation with subnational governments on foreign affairs issues."[56] Kuznetsov has also pointed out that the Soviet constitution of 1936 had earlier allowed its former republics to exercise external relations with foreign states on various issues including defence policies.[57]

2. **Federalist:** Scholars like Duchacek, Soldatos and Kincaid have argued that the presence of subnational governments in international affairs will enhance the federalist structure as it can rationalise the decision-making process and further democratise the foreign policy.[58] One of the scholars, Ronald Atkey, has insisted that "a central government should delegate responsibilities to subnational governments as 'component units' that are relatively competent to excel performance level in certain issues."[59] This emphasises the decentralisation of issues that concern the local and regional government. Atkey also suggests that "it is necessary for these subnational external activities to function under the guidance of the central government in order to safeguard national interests."[60]

   Therefore, it is advised that subnational governments should conduct relations with foreign states on low politics issues, such as education, poverty, health security, climate change, urban development etc. For example, in 1983, the US National League of Cities, under a cooperative framework of major and minor cities, organised a conference in San Antonio to brief administrators on the need of developing the cities' foreign relations.[61]

   The study of paradiplomacy also expanded in Latin America and Asia. In 2005, Purnendra Jain published a monograph on Japan's subnational government in international affairs.[62] Later, Chinese provinces were also studied as potential players in international relations. This emerging trend challenged the traditional notion of paradiplomacy as the concept was relevant only to federal and quasi-federal states, but not to unitary nations like Japan and non-democratic countries like China.

3. **Nationalism**: Regions such as Quebec, Flanders, Wallonia, Catalonia and the Basque, where paradiplomacy is most active, share a common trait—nationalism.[63] Taking account of these regions, two notable scholars, Andre Lecours and Luis Moreno, have stated that paradiplomacy and nationalism are interrelated through three processes.[64] The first process is

identity construction and consolidation through mechanisms like cultural exchange, institutional development and socio-economic transformation, which will further nurture the idea of a national community.

The second process is definition and "articulation of regional/group interests, which means the promotion of common goods based on cultural preservation that is inherent in nationalist movements and is reflected in domestic and international politics."[65] For instance, in 1991, Baden-Württemberg established a joint commission with a Hungarian state based on strong ethnic ties with the Danube Swabian people. Further, the French region of Brittany has a partnership with Wales to promote their shared Celtic culture.[66]

The third process is political and territorial mobilisation, which is loosely related to paradiplomacy, but from the nationalist perspective, "it is a kind of power politics that focuses on the mobilisation of societies based on the actualisation of their territorial commonness."[67] Moreover, there is a common assumption that central governments would certainly oppose paradiplomacy due to such national aspirations. Yet, in certain cases, subnational activities allow the national government to extract more opportunities in the country's domestic affairs. For instance, in 2004, the Mexican government recognised the Chiapas agreement with the EU, through which it received €15 million to assist the poverty-ridden indigenous people who lived in the Lacandon jungle.[68] This suggests that the division between the regional and central authorities cannot be predetermined based on a zero-sum game.

4. **International:** The present scenario of world politics renders the international arena as a marketplace, where bargaining, i.e., cooperation through transnational relations outweighs the zero-sum game between the actors and non-actors, such as NGOs, MNCs and subnational governments.[69] From the liberalists' perspective, the regions set out to be the transnational actors in international relations, resulting in the strengthening of subnational identities.[70] Therefore, such transnational relations, i.e., paradiplomacy, cannot flourish in authoritarian societies. Within the realist viewpoint, such transnational actors in world politics are the rational will of states as they act globally to maximise benefits for national interests. For instance, Chinese provinces, such as Guangdong,

Shanghai or Tianjin have engaged with foreign nations as a part of the diplomatic strategy, 'Zhoubian', which was initiated after the Tiananmen crisis[71].

Such instances indicate that paradiplomacy is an instrument for the central government to prevent negative international attitudes.[72] Further, the constructivist approach provides a middle ground to the liberalist and realist perception of transnational relations. Alexander Wendt has emphasised that the realist needs to acknowledge the potential role of non-state actors in its state-centric model.[73] In addition, Early Fry has remarked that the "texts in international relations either maintain a state-centric emphasis or give some credence to non-state actors, such as multinational corporations, without pinpointing the role that non-central governments play in the international arena."[74] The concept of paradiplomacy requires extensive research among scholars to perceive it as an international theory within the academic discourse.

5. **Border Studies**: Paradiplomacy, under this dimension, is comprehended through transborder cooperation of subnational agreements. For instance, the ORU–FOGAR (United Nations Region Organization/ Forum of Regional Governments and Global Association of Regions) organised a seminar in Montevideo, titled "The Subnational Governments in the Framework of Regional Integration Processes", to address border cooperation among the local and regional administration and private entities.[75] This is also known as transborder diplomacy, which focuses on the contribution of subnational governments in international affairs at the grassroot level. Within this context, subnational governments, national government and supranational institutions arrive at a mutual understanding that provides opportunities for economic, social and cultural development through the establishment of 'regional corridors'.[76] For instance, the Maputo Development Corridor is a trade route that links the landlocked and northeast provinces of South Africa to Maputo, the capital of Mozambique. The Maputo corridor has bilateral policies with subnational governments supported by private and public investments.[77] These policies are driven by sustainable growth and regional development.
6. **Globalisation**: Paradiplomacy seems to be a "consequence of globalisation processes and it possesses a dualistic nature: constituent

diplomacy is enabled by globalisation and simultaneously, paradiplomacy further accelerates globalisation."[78] Globalisation has extensively revolutionised global economics through free movement of capital, labour and technologies and transnational regimes, such as WTO and NAFTA. Moreover, MNCs such as Google and Microsoft, with their foreign investments and global exports, have enhanced their economic power within national governments and supranational bodies as well as subnational governments. Another aspect that connects paradiplomacy and globalisation has been highlighted by Michael Keating that "modern communication technology and the dominance of a global culture originating largely in the United States have eroded national cultures and the role of states in promoting and protecting them."[79] He further mentions that states today do not have "adequate resources to resist cultural globalisation and thus, regions possess a strong desire to protect their cultural heritage by actively promoting their identity in the international arena, such as Quebec and Basque country."[80] Due to cultural globalisation, states have large diasporas of communities living abroad. For example, the Mexican states of Michoacán, Guanajuato and Puebla Zacatecas have foreign offices in New York, California, Illinois and Texas to organise social and cultural events for their Mexican immigrants.[81] Thus, economic globalisation and cultural globalisation are two important aspects that determine the relationship between paradiplomacy and globalisation.

7. **International Security and Geopolitical Approach**: According to Noah Carnago, paradiplomacy is an effective mechanism to deal with emerging challenges under international security pertaining to ethnic conflicts, control of migration and administration of ecological issues.[82] Noe has stated that:

> "The problem of the Austrian Tyrol and the German speaking minority of Bolzano have similar characteristics but have evolved very differently. In this case, barriers to cross-border contacts were imposed in the post-war period by the Italian government. Its promises to grant autonomy to Bolzano were diluted by the creation of the Trentino-Alto Adige region. The discontent of

> the Austrian minority led to Austria bringing up the issue in the UN in the early 1970s. This pressure, together with the incipient emergence of terrorism, finally persuaded the Italian government to recognise special rights for the minority of Bolzano."[83]

At the end of the decade, tolerance was developed by building strong relations among the Tyrolese people from both sides. Due to this, the relation between Austria and Italy improved, which resulted in the "configuration of one of the most unusual expressions of the ethno-political dimension of foreign affairs. Further, both the governments held periodic joint meetings of provincial chambers belonging to different states."[84] In terms of ecological issues, the Council of the Great Lakes, in 2011, institutionalised cross-border cooperation between the Canadian provinces and USA for the preservation of 20 per cent of the world's fresh water supplies.[85]

8. **Global Economy**: The population shift from rural to urban areas has caused urbanisation, which has ultimately energised cities to become active players in the global economy. The 'global cities' and 'megacities' have become the vital stakeholders in generating global GDP. Moreover, the establishment of foreign offices, financial and technical assistance and investment in international trade shows enduring partnerships among the local and foreign entrepreneurs. This approach has enabled cities and regional governments to expand their cultural, social and economic linkages across the nation. The role of cities in the global economy has been explored in detail subsequently.
9. **Environmental**: Supranational bodies, such as the EU, UN and NAFTA have played major roles in framing global sustainable development policies. The practical implementation of these environmental policies has also taken place at the regional level under the parameters of 'green' paradiplomacy. In this context, cities and states have created a positive trend to combat issues of climate change. For instance, California has its own 'climate diplomacy' with some Chinese provinces and Quebec to curb carbon emissions.[86]

   In 2002, the Network of Regional Governments for Sustainable Development was established to design a sustainable development policy.[87] It had 50 members. The Cities Climate Leadership Group (C40) is a network of megacities that addresses issues of climate change, such as greenhouse gas emissions through sustainable action.[88] The international community has also acknowledged such efforts made by regional governments at an international forum. In 2013, the UN Secretariat awarded the 'Water for Life'[89] UN-Water Best Practices award to Kumamoto city in Japan for supplying all drinking water with natural groundwater. The Green Star Awards is another initiative by Green Cross International that recognises individuals or organisations that have made significant efforts to prevent, prepare for and respond to urgent environmental issues. It was awarded to Masahide Matsumoto, the mayor of Katsurao village near Fukushima in Japan, in 2013. The Leadership Award by the World Green Building Council acknowledges the leadership of local governments in mitigating environmental impact. It was awarded to Seoul, Vancouver, Abu Dhabi and Christchurch.[90]

10. **Traditional Diplomacy**: The traditional notion of diplomacy is confined to relations between sovereign states. But the contemporary forms of diplomacy, such as celebrity diplomacy, guerilla diplomacy, city diplomacy, paradiplomacy etc. require IR theorists to reevaluate the interaction between the state and non-state actors within the international environment. However, due to inadequate study, paradiplomacy discourse in this dimension is yet to be fully shaped as a constructive approach. This dimension lacks a theoretical framework that could incorporate the evolving concepts of diplomacy. Moreover, comparative research is needed to analyse the external activities of subnational governments.
11. **Separatists/Non-recognised States**: This dimension focuses on the paradiplomatic practices of subnational entities that are *de jure* 'subnational', but are *de facto* 'sovereign nations'. Taiwan, Kosovo, Abkhazia, South Ossetia, Northern Cyprus, Nagorno-Karabakh and Transnistria are classic examples of such subnational entities. After the fall of the USSR and Yugoslavia, the failure of communist regimes has contributed to the problems of *de facto* nations in global affairs due to an upsurge in ethnic conflicts and territorial claims. The subnational governments, such as Kosovo, Abkhazia etc. have struggled for international recognition for statehood.[91] For instance, Taiwan is considered by many as a non-

recognised state. Under the 'One China'[92] policy, a national government that develops diplomatic relations with China has to automatically break its relations with Taiwan, due to which Taiwan has limited official recognition. However, Taipei is an active player in the international arena through paradiplomacy, which in this case, is similar to the traditional notion of diplomacy.[93] Under the pretext of paradiplomacy, Taiwan has formal relations with 29 countries and has a large number of foreign offices based on trade, culture and tourism.[94] The case of Taiwan highlights the essence of paradiplomacy in non-recognised states. The external activities of regions struggling for international recognition can be considered as *de jure* paradiplomacy, but *de facto,* it is similar to sovereign state diplomacy.[95] Thus, under this dimension, paradiplomacy is strictly linked to economic, cultural and geopolitical determinants and not the political issues within the central government and subnational government.

As Aguirre points out, "At the end of the 20th century, it became obvious that there exist diverse autonomous international activities that are connected with the day-to-day political responsibilities of local democratic governmental authorities and people's vital interests. These activities address the economic, social, ecological, cultural and normative issues of modern democracies. This is one more consequence of the increasingly complex and diverse internalisation of local public policies—those policies which are closer to the citizens. In a way, it is one more consequence of the local international response to the unavoidable challenge of the contemporary process of localisation of international relations."[96]

Notes

1. Alexander S. Kuznetsov, *Theory and Practice of Paradiplomacy*, ed. Markus Kornprobst Corneliu Bjola, Subnational Governments in International Affairs (London, New York: Routledge, 2015), p. 35.
2. Ibid., p. 102.
3. Ibid.
4. Tavares, *Paradiplomacy: Cities and States as Global Players.*
5. Ratna, T. (2013, November 10). *Paradiplomacy: A New Way for Indian Foreign Policy?* Retrieved from The Diplomat: https://thediplomat.com/2013/11/paradiplomacy-a-new-way-for-indian-foreign-policy/

6. Prime Minister's Office, "Text of Prime Minister's Inaugural Address at Delhi Economics Conclave," Press Information Bureau, Government of India, November 6, 2015, accessed June 25, 2016, http://pib.nic.in/newsite/PrintRelease .aspx?relid=130283.
7. MEA, "V. K. Singh on Q No.687 Separate Division for Centre-State Relations," ed. Ministry of State (Government of India, 2014).
8. FSI, "State Specialization by Ifs Ots of 2014 Batch," (Foreign Service Institute: Government of India, 2015).
9. Tavares, *Paradiplomacy: Cities and States as Global Players*, p. 229.
10. "Forget the Nation-State: Cities Will Transform the Way We Conduct Foreign Affairs," World Economic Forum, https://www.weforum.org/agenda/2016/10/forget-the-nation-state-cities-will-transform-the-way-we-conduct-foreign-affairs/. (2016).
11. Kuznetsov, *Theory and Practice of Paradiplomacy*.
12. Ibid.
13. Mathieu Pigeon, "The Quiet Revolution," McCord Museum, http://collections.musee-mccord.qc.ca/scripts/explore.php?Lang=1&elementid=109__true&tableid=11&tablename=theme&contentlong.
14. Kuznetsov, *Theory and Practice of Paradiplomacy*.
15. Eugene Boyd, "American Federalism, 1776 to 1997: Significant Events," https://usa.usembassy.de/, https://usa.usembassy.de/etexts/gov/federal.htm.
16. Ibid.
17. Kuznetsov, *Theory and Practice of Paradiplomacy*, p. 35.
18. Ivo Duchacek, "The International Dimension of Subnational Self-Government," *Publius: The Journal of Federalism* (1984).
19. Ibid., p. 10.
20. Tavares, *Paradiplomacy: Cities and States as Global Players*, p. 8.
21. Kuznetsov, *Theory and Practice of Paradiplomacy*, p. 26.
22. Ibid.
23. Butler related Paradiplomacy with secret negotiations that take place within the shadow of official diplomacy.
24. Kuznetsov, *Theory and Practice of Paradiplomacy*.
25. Ibid., p. 27.
26. Duchacek, "The International Dimension of Subnational Self-Government," p. 5.
27. Also known as Micro-diplomacy.
28. Duchacek, "The International Dimension of Subnational Self-Government," p. 9.
29. Ibid., p. 2.
30. Kuznetsov, *Theory and Practice of Paradiplomacy*, p. 27.

31. Non-central Government (NCG) is synonymous to regional and local governments.
32. The examples of protodiplomacy as provided by Duchacek are Quebec in Canada, non-recognized states after the fall of USSR such as Yugoslavia, Abkhaiza, South Ossetia, Kosovo or Nagorno-Karabakh. For the research purpose protodiplomacy shall not be used as a term to describe the regional activities with a separatist message. Rather it shall be used under the umbrella term of 'paradiplomacy'.
33. Kuznetsov, *Theory and Practice of Paradiplomacy*, p. 37.
34. Jana Deforche Peter Bursens, "Going Beyond Paradiplomacy? Adding Historical Institutionalism to Account for Regional Foreign Policy Competences," *The Hague Journal of Diplomacy* 5 (2010).
35. Kuznetsov, *Theory and Practice of Paradiplomacy*, p. 28.
36. John Kincaid, "Foreign Relations of Sub-National Units", https://forumfed.org/, http://www.forumfed.org/pubs/StG-Kincaid.pdf.
37. Kuznetsov, *Theory and Practice of Paradiplomacy*, p. 28.
38. Ibid., p. 29.
39. John Kincaid, "Roles of Constituent Governments", http://www.forumfed.org/, http://www.forumfed.org/libdocs/ForRelCU01/924-FRCU0105-int-kincaid.pdf.
40. Duchacek, "The International Dimension of Subnational Self-Government," p. 3.
41. EU, "European Committee of the Regions (Cor)," https://european-union.europa.eu/, https://european-union.europa.eu/institutions-law-budget/institutions-and-bodies/institutions-and-bodies-profiles/cor_en.
42. Ibid.
43. Interreg Europe, "What Is Interreg Europe?," https://www.interregeurope.eu/, https://www.interregeurope.eu/what-is-interreg-europe.
44. Kuznetsov, *Theory and Practice of Paradiplomacy*, p. 24.
45. Ibid., p. 29.
46. Renato Balbim, "The Workers' Party Contribution to the City Diplomacy in Brazil. A Local-Global Ideology," *Public Diplomacy of Rising and Regional Powers* 3, no. 3 (2018).
47. Tavares, *Paradiplomacy: Cities and States as Global Players*, p. 9.
48. Iñaki Aguirre, "Making Sense of Paradiplomacy? An Intertextual Enquiry About a Concept in Search of a Definition," *Regional and Federal Studies* (2009).
49. Ibid., p. 17.
50. Ibid., p. 20.
51. Newly coined terminologies and words.
52. Kuznetsov, *Theory and Practice of Paradiplomacy*, p. 25.
53. Ibid., p. 30.

54. Ibid., p. 53.
55. Kanat Ydyrys Aidarbek Amirbek, "Education and Soft Power: Analysis as an Instrument of Foreign Policy," *Procedia - Social and Behavioral Sciences* 143 (2014).
56. J. Trone, *Federal Constitutions and International Relations* (University of Queensland Press, 2001).
57. Kuznetsov, *Theory and Practice of Paradiplomacy*, p. 54.
58. Ibid., p. 64.
59. Ronald G. Atkey, "The Role of Provinces in International Affairs," *International Journal* 26, no. 1 (1971).
60. Kuznetsov, *Theory and Practice of Paradiplomacy.*
61. Duchacek, "The International Dimension of Subnational Self-Government," p. 3.
62. Purnendra Jain, *Japan's Subnational Governments in International Affairs*, 1st ed. (London: Routledge, 2005).
63. Kuznetsov, *Theory and Practice of Paradiplomacy*, p. 66.
64. Luis Moreno André Lecours, "Paradiplomacy: A Nation-Building Strategy? A Reference to the Basque Country," in *The Conditions of Diversity in Multinational Democracies*, ed. Montserrat Guibernau Alain Gagnon, François Rocher (The Institute for Research on Public Policy Canada, 2003).
65. Kuznetsov, *Theory and Practice of Paradiplomacy*, p. 67.
66. Tavares, *Paradiplomacy: Cities and States as Global Players*, p. 45.
67. Kuznetsov, *Theory and Practice of Paradiplomacy.*
68. Tavares, *Paradiplomacy: Cities and States as Global Players.*
69. Kuznetsov, *Theory and Practice of Paradiplomacy*, p. 71.
70. Ibid., p. 72.
71. The Tiananmen Square protest of 1989 was led by pro-democratic protesters to bring political and economic reforms in China.
72. Kuznetsov, *Theory and Practice of Paradiplomacy*, p. 74.
73. Alexander Wendt, "Collective Identity Information and the International State," *American Political Science Review* 88, no. 2 (1994).
74. Kuznetsov, *Theory and Practice of Paradiplomacy*, p. 69.
75. ORU-FOGAR, "The Role of Cross-Border Cooperation," ORU-FOGAR, http://www.regionsunies-fogar.org/en/join-oru/opinion-articles/109-the-role-of-cross-border-cooperation.
76. Tavares, *Paradiplomacy: Cities and States as Global Players*, p. 46.
77. mcli.co.za, "Maputo Development Corridor," http://www.mcli.co.za/maputo-development-corridor/.
78. Kuznetsov, *Theory and Practice of Paradiplomacy*, p. 77.
79. Ibid.

80. Ibid.
81. Tavares, *Paradiplomacy: Cities and States as Global Players*, p. 45.
82. Kuznetsov, *Theory and Practice of Paradiplomacy*, p. 78.
83. Noe Carnago, *Diplomacy and Paradiplomacy in the Redefinition of International Security: Dimensions of Conflict and Cooperation,* ed. Michael Keating Francisco Aldecoa, Paradiplomacy in Action: The Foreign Relations of Subnational Governments (New York: Routledge Taylor and Francis Group, 2013), p. 43.
84. Ibid.
85. councilgreatlakesregion.org, "General Info," Council of the Great Lakes Region https://councilgreatlakesregion.org/about-cglr/.
86. Tavares, *Paradiplomacy: Cities and States as Global Players*, p. 37.
87. Kuznetsov, *Theory and Practice of Paradiplomacy*, p. 83.
88. C40, "C40 Cities Climate Leadership Group", http://www.c40.org/.
89. Award aims to acknowledge and promote efforts to fulfill international commitments made on water and sanitation- related issues by 2015.
90. Tavares, *Paradiplomacy: Cities and States as Global Players*, p. 113.
91. Kuznetsov, *Theory and Practice of Paradiplomacy*, p. 88.
92. The One- China principle is the position held by the People's Republic of China that there is only one sovereign state under the name 'China', and Taiwan is a part of China.
93. Kuznetsov, *Theory and Practice of Paradiplomacy*, p. 89.
94. Eric Harwit, "Taiwan's Foreign Economic Relations with Developing Nations: A Case Study of Its Ties with Palau," *The Contemporary Pacific* 12, no. 2 (2000).
95. Kuznetsov, *Theory and Practice of Paradiplomacy*, p. 91.
96. Aguirre, "Making Sense of Paradiplomacy? An Intertextual Enquiry About a Concept in Search of a Definition," p. 23.

2

Evolution of Paradiplomacy

The history of the engagement of cities and regions with foreign countries can be traced back to the Greek city-states of Athens, Corinth, Thebes and Sparta and the ancient Egyptian city-states of Thebes and Memphis. In the pre-Columbian era, many Mesoamerican cities, such as Chichen Itza, Tikal, Monte Albán and Tenochtitlan developed relations with foreign countries. Other such examples include the Central Asian cities of the Silk Road and the Viking colonial cities in medieval Ireland. Later, in the 15th century, Milan, under the Italian condottiere, Francesco Sforza, played a leading role in launching permanent embassies in the city-states of northern Italy. These examples can loosely characterise the presence of paradiplomacy 5000 years ago.[1]

Further, in the late 19th century, the colonies under British rule acted as agent generals in London and Paris, such as Victoria in 1857[2], South Australia in 1858, Queensland in 1869, Quebec in 1882, Tasmania in 1886 and Western Australia in 1891. The notion of paradiplomacy evolved in the 20th century when local governments started taking an interest in international exchanges.[3] For example, in 1911, the province of Quebec opened its first 'commercial' office in Britain followed by Brussels in 1915.[4] In 1907, São Paulo in Brazil signed an agreement with Japan concerning thousands of Japanese immigrants in the region.[5] This is considered as the first international agreement that was signed by a substate. São Paulo currently hosts the largest Japanese diaspora in the world.

In 1913, the International Union of Local Authorities (IULA) was set up in the Netherlands "to promote democratic local self-government of emerging European cities."[6] During the post-war period, IULA held a congress in

Paris in 1947, where a group of French and German mayors founded the Union International des Maires to establish peace between the countries. Currently, the IULA has local government members present in 100 countries.[7] Furthermore, the Council of European Municipalities was established with representative offices in Austria, Belgium, Germany, France, Great Britain, Luxemburg, Italy, the Netherlands, Switzerland and Spain.[8] Under this, an assembly of 50 mayors drafted policies and guidelines, which led to the conclusion of several town-twinning agreements among the European cities. Later, in 1950, President Eisenhower adopted a similar approach in the US by launching sister-city agreements.[9] Gradually, in the 1960s, foreign affairs governing bodies were being established at the subnational level. For example, in 1967, the Legislative Assembly of Quebec established the Ministry of Intergovernmental Relations, which became the first institutional body where a region like Quebec could foster its international relations.

In 1971, the Association of European Border Regions was created based on the geographical proximity of the regions. Other such forums in Europe include the Conference of Peripheral Maritime Region in 1973 and the European Industrial Regions Association (EIRA) in 2002[10]. The EIRA focused on the common interests of the bordering regions represented by national and international parliaments, bodies, authorities and institutions. Further, in 1988, the Four Motors for Europe, within the framework of the EU, brought forth an international dimension among the leading regional economies of Baden-Württemberg, Catalonia, Lombardy and Rhône-Alpes. During this period, the first high-level discussions were held at the 25th Congress of the Communist Party of the Soviet Union, which highlighted the active participation of regional leaders in foreign issues. However, such issues were ad hoc and confined to cultural exchanges and foreign investments.

In the late 20th century, the process of globalisation had internationalised domestic affairs. This was also known as 'glocalisation'. The integrated global economy caused the states to cooperate with MNCs, trade unions, international organisations, international non-governmental organisations (INGOs) and social movements. Moreover, in 1980, the political and economic effects of globalisation urged European subnational entities to integrate in the global markets. Under this concept of 'new regionalism', they were granted constitutional and institutional freedom to broaden their diplomatic activities based on the judicial standards set by the EU.[11] For instance, up till 1990, Belgium's foreign policy of regions was limited to the cultural and educational domains. But, later, the St. Michael Agreement in September 1992 brought about constitutional reforms, which laid the foundation of a federal state in Belgium. These reforms further enabled the expansion of external relations within the region.[12]

The presence of paradiplomacy was felt mostly in federal countries, such as Canada, Germany, Belgium, Switzerland, Australia and the US and also in some unitary countries like Spain and France. But, paradiplomacy was a breakthrough in the 21st century due to its noteworthy practices in the substates of Argentina, Brazil, Chile, China, India, Japan, Mexico, Russia and South Africa. At present, there are 125 multilateral networks and forums of subnational governments that focus on issues such as sustainable development, culture, education and urban management, as listed in Appendix A.[13] They include prominent organisations such as the ORU-FOGAR in 2009 and the World Council of the United Cities and Local Governments (UCLG) in 2010. In 2015, the first strategic partnership was established with the European Commission, signed by the Association of Francophone Mayors (AIMF), Commonwealth Local Government Forum (CLGF), CEMR, UCLG and UCLG Africa. The partnership acknowledged subnational governments' role in addressing global agendas through the policy-making and decision-making processes.

The Four Stages of Paradiplomacy

Since the 20th century, the cities have engaged in paradiplomatic activities in diverse areas. One needs to acknowledge that paradiplomacy does not have a precise definition as it is a multi-layered term. The evolution of paradiplomacy can be further explained in four stages as follows:

1930—Ceremonial Diplomacy

Ceremonial diplomacy is where subnational entities host conferences and meetings with non-binding agreements in which subnational governments are not legally obliged to carry out the paradiplomatic activities. Twin town or sister-state agreements are a kind of "non-binding cooperative arrangement made between subnational governments in geographically and politically distinct areas to promote cultural and commercial ties."[14] The initial phase of town-twinning occurred in 836 A.D. between Paderborn (Germany) and Le Mans (France).[15] Toledo in North America was the first city to develop a sister-city arrangement with Toledo in Spain.[16] The concept of town-twinning re-emerged after World War II between the EU member-states and the countries of Central and Eastern Europe. The first case of twinning was started in 1930 between one German and one Austrian partner.[17] As a part of the EU integration process, the Bristol Council concluded a town-twinning agreement with Hanover in 1947.[18] A similar approach was undertaken by Bonn and Oxford, followed by Reading and Düsseldorf.[19] Later, in 1950, the first German-French twinning took place between Montbéliard and Ludwigsburg.[20] Today, town-twinning is a defining aspect of Europe due to the increasing coordination and collaboration between municipalities. Currently, Europe has about 1000 friendship agreements. Such partnerships have strengthened cooperation between the towns and mutual understanding between their citizens.[21] In 2006, the EU established the 'Europe for Citizens' programme, which provided a legal framework for the active involvement of citizens and civil society organisations in the European integration process. As of 2015, the programme has invested €3.9 million and further endorsed 240 town-twinning initiatives.[22]

In the US and Japan, the first sister-city agreement was signed in 1955 between Saint Paul (Minnesota) and Nagasaki.[23] In 1956, under the programme of the National League of Cities, Eisenhower promoted the concept of citizen diplomacy to strengthen bonds between people from different cities. This initiative was later headed by the Sister Cities International in 1967.[24] Town-twinning agreements are also prevalent among Asian countries, such as China, India and Japan. Chinese subnational governments have set up 2,570 sister- city agreements.[25] The president of the Philippines, Gloria Macapagal Arroyo, at the Third Philippine International Sisterhood and Twinning Association in 2009, stated that town- twinning boosts the economy through the exchange of ideas, technology, services and manpower due to its ceremonial approach.[26]

Nevertheless, the significance of town- twinning agreements is diminishing in certain aspects as subnational governments gain less opportunities and political willingness. For example, in 2006, New York desisted from signing any further sister agreements; rather, it suggested that linkages with foreign cities should be galvanised through New York City Global Partners, Inc.[27] Since these agreements are non-binding in nature, they lack concrete results as compared to national bilateral agreements. In 2011, São Paulo conducted only those international cooperation agreements that carried political substance and robust commitments.[28] In 2014, a first city-to-city agreement was signed between the mayors of Chicago and Mexico at the Global Cities Economic Partnership. The agreement led to a series of joint ventures in trade and investment and further boosted innovation, human capital and education to increase job prospects.[29]

1960—Sovereign Diplomacy

As discussed earlier, paradiplomacy, under this stage, is conceived as 'protodiplomacy', a term that refers to "the conduct of international relations by a non-central government that aims at establishing a full sovereign state."[30] The inclusion of provinces in foreign affairs, secularisation of society and the creation of a welfare state were considered as crucial modules of the modernisation of a state. Here, paradiplomacy is perceived as normal activity, reflecting the degree of autonomy given to a state, whereas protodiplomacy is considered as illegitimate or dangerous to the integrity of the state. Quebec is a classic example of protodiplomacy. The Quiet Revolution of Quebec in the 1960s was a period of intense socio-political and socio-cultural change. Moreover, Canada is the sole country that recognises the right to secede from the federation.[31] Other such examples include Catalonia and Basque (Spain), Flanders and Wallonia (Belgium), the Free State of Bavaria (Germany), Scotland (UK), Tatarstan (Russia), Transnistria (Moldava), Puntland and Somaliland (Somalia).[32] These regions claim that subnational governments should become fully responsible for their own foreign policy.

1970—Single-Themed Diplomacy

This diplomacy implicates/implies cross-border cooperation on specific issues, such as economic growth and environment. As a result, various MoUs were concluded among neighbouring states since the 1980s, such as Alberta and Montana (1985), Manitoba and Minnesota (1988), British Columbia and Washington State (1992), Ontario and New York (2001), Michigan and New York (2002) and Quebec and New York (2002).[33] The benefits of transborder cooperation have eased the relations between the cities and states of neighbouring countries. Eventually, multilateral bodies, such as the Pacific Northwest Economic Region (1991) that includes the states of North America and Canada,[34,35] were created to strengthen this bilateral transborder cooperation.[36, 37] Other examples include the Conference of New England Governors and Eastern Canadian Premiers (1973), Council of Great Lakes Governors (1983) and the Great Lakes and St. Lawrence Cities Initiative (2003).[38] In 1988, the two consecutive oil spills near the Pacific coast received negligible reaction from the federal governments, which led British Columbia, Alaska, Washington and Oregon to develop a Task Force to integrate their technical, financial and human resources to overcome ecological disasters along their coast.[39] Furthermore, the silence of the federal governments caused Pennsylvania, Illinois, Ohio, Wisconsin, New York, Minnesota, Quebec and Ontario to develop cooperation to undertake measures against acid rain and further such deterioration of the Great Lakes.[40] In Europe, the Conference of Peripheral and Maritime Regions (1970) is the largest territorial lobby, represented by 160 regions.[41] Tavares has mentioned that "the involvement of governors of bordering states in foreign policy is necessary to handle the issues of immigration and border security."[42] Moreover, in the areas of trade and investment, Australian states, such as New South Wales, Queensland, Victoria and Western Australia have their own trade missions and investment policies.[43] For instance, Trade and Investment Queensland has representative offices in 14 regions. Under this diplomacy, political agendas are not dealt with by subnational governments.[44]

2000—Global Paradiplomacy

Global paradiplomacy encourages subnational governments to participate in international debates and engage beyond their geographical proximities, in diverse areas ranging from environment to culture, from infrastructure to R&D and from education to trade and investment promotion. A considerable number of subnational governments from China, Brazil, Germany, Canada and France are prominent examples of global paradiplomacy. In Canada, along with Quebec, all 10 provincial governments have formed a separate ministry to manage their external relations.[45] They also have overseas offices that function according to their own policies to defend their interests. According to the World Economic Forum, California is the sixth largest economy in the world, surpassing France, India, Italy and Brazil.[46] California's global leadership in climate diplomacy, started by Arnold Schwarzenegger, was recognised by the Chinese environmental protection minister, Zhou Shengxian, which led to a non-binding agreement to reduce smog and greenhouse gas (GHG) emissions. California and Quebec took a joint step towards linking carbon markets—the Western Climate initiative. As per the report of the American Enterprise Institute (AEI), Texas was the 10th largest economy in the world, with a $1.55 trillion GDP in 2015, slightly higher than Canada.[47] Such instances demonstrate that subnational governments and cities can no longer be dependent on national ministries to carry out their external activities. The importance of cities in the global GDP is explored in subsequence.

The concept of paradiplomacy within academic study is not yet clearly defined, but its practice is notable across the globe. Globalisation has penetrated the traditional methods of the diplomatic affairs of states. This chapter attempted to study how paradiplomacy, as a concept, became a prominent practice in the wake of globalisation among federal countries, such as Austria, Belgium, Canada, Germany, Switzerland and the US and unitary countries like France and Spain. The chapter implies that the practice of paradiplomacy does not disturb states as the primary actors in international politics, but changes the course and style of interaction between and among states. Paradiplomacy has indeed emerged as an extension of modern diplomatic studies. It is a concept that does not challenge the traditional notion of diplomacy; rather, it broadens the scope of diplomatic studies and its practice in international relations. The term 'parallel diplomacy', an abbreviation of paradiplomacy, seems to have wrong connotation. It is rather a supplementary diplomacy; a furtherance of national diplomacy.

Notes

1. Tavares, *Paradiplomacy: Cities and States as Global Players*, p. 10.
2. In March 1857 Hugh Childers was elected Victoria's first agent general in London. He continued in the office until the end of 1857 but remained Victoria's informal representative in England until 1862, when he was again appointed officially.
3. Tavares, *Paradiplomacy: Cities and States as Global Players*, p. 11.

4. Chris Kukucha, "Development Cooperation and Multilateralism: The Alberta Experience," http://www.forumfed.org/, http://www.forumfed.org/libdocs/2009/2008-09-18-Kukucha.pdf.
5. Junichi Goto, "Latin Americans of Japanese Origin (Nikkeijin) "worldbank.org, https://documents1.worldbank.org/curated/en/604121468020036821/pdf/wps4203.pdf.
6. UNESCWA, "International Union of Local Authorities," https://archive.unescwa.org/, https://archive.unescwa.org/international-union-local-authorities.
7. City Mayors: IULA, "Iula Promotes Democratic Local Governments Worldwide," http://www.citymayors.com/features/iula.html.
8. CEMR, "Town Twinning," European section of United Cities and Local Governments, http://www.ccre.org/en/activites/view/9.
9. sistercities.org, "Mission and History," http://www.sistercities.org/mission-and-history.
10. The European Regions of Industrial Technology and the Conference and Association of Steel Territories were merged in 2002 as the European Industrial Regions Association.
11. Stephen Buzdugan, "New Regionalism," https://www.britannica.com/, https://www.britannica.com/topic/new-regionalism.
12. Tavares, *Paradiplomacy: Cities and States as Global Players*, p. 14.
13. Ibid.
14. Ibid., p. 29.
15. www.highland.gov.uk, "The City of Inverness Town Twinning Committee" The Highland Council, https://web.archive.org/web/20101231083242/http://www.highland.gov.uk/NR/rdonlyres/1C07A195-EF04-454D-81B8-ADAEE15058FC/0/ICC9908.pdf.
16. Toledo Sister-Cities, "Toledo, Spain," http://www.toledosistercities.org/, http://www.toledosistercities.org/sistercities/toledo-spain/.
17. Mr Örtengren, "Development of Town Twinning since 1989 " https://ec.europa.eu/, https://ec.europa.eu/citizenship/pdf/doc374_en.pdf.
18. bristol.gov.uk, "Twinning," Bristol City Council, https://www.bristol.gov.uk/museums-parks-sports-culture/twinning.
19. Tavares, *Paradiplomacy: Cities and States as Global Players*.
20. ludwigsburg.de, "Ludwigsburg and Its Partner Cities," https://www.ludwigsburg.de/, https://www.ludwigsburg.de/site/Ludwigsburg-Internet-2020/get/params_E645929329/17943014/Ludwigsburg%20and%20its%20partner%20cities.pdf.
21. Tavares, *Paradiplomacy: Cities and States as Global Players*, p. 30.
22. Ibid.

23. CLAIR, "Local Government International Exchange," Council of Local Authorities of International Relation, http://www.clair.or.jp/e/exchange/shimai/qanda.html.
24. sistercities.org, "About Sister Cities International," Sister Cities International, https://sistercities.org/about-us/.
25. ChinaDaily, "This Day, That Year: June 24," www.chinadaily.com.cn/, https://www.chinadaily.com.cn/m/tianjinport/2019-06/24/content_37483915.htm#:~:text=On%20June%2024%2C%201973%2C%20Tianjin,for%20Friendship%20with%20Foreign%20Countries.
26. officialgazette.gov.ph, "Speech of President Arroyo During the 3rd Philippine International Sisterhood and Twinning Association, Inc. (Phista) Region Iv-a (Calabarzon) Chapter Assembly Cum Seminar Workshop and 1st Tourism Summit," Official Gazette, https://www.officialgazette.gov.ph/2009/10/22/speech-of-president-arroyo-during-the-3rd-philippine-international-sisterhood-and-twinning-association-inc-phista-region-iv-a-calabarzon-chapter-assembly-cum-seminar-workshop-and-1st-tourism-sum/.
27. Tavares, *Paradiplomacy: Cities and States as Global Players*. New York City Global Partners is a network of over one hundred cities that meet annually and is led by the Mayor's Office for International Affairs.
28. Ibid.
29. brookings.edu, "México City and Chicago Announce Innovative Economic Partnership," (Global Cities Initiative: Brookings, 2013).
30. Tavares, *Paradiplomacy: Cities and States as Global Players*, p. 38.
31. Supreme Court of Canada, "Reference Re Secession of Quebec," https://scc-csc.lexum.com/, https://scc-csc.lexum.com/scc-csc/scc-csc/en/item/1643/index.do.
32. Tavares, *Paradiplomacy: Cities and States as Global Players*.
33. Ibid.
34. The states include British Columbia, Alberta, Yukon and the states of Alaska, Idaho, Montana, Oregon, and Washington.
35. Tavares, *Paradiplomacy: Cities and States as Global Players*.
36. The states include British Columbia, Alberta, Yukon and the states of Alaska, Idaho, Montana, Oregon, and Washington.
37. Tavares, *Paradiplomacy: Cities and States as Global Players*.
38 Ibid.
39. Sarah Brace, "25 Years of Collaboration: The Pacific States/British Columbia Oil Spill Task Force 1989–2014", https://meridian.allenpress.com/.
40. epa.gov, "Great Lakes Restoration Initiative Action Plan Iii Fiscal Year 2020 - Fiscal Year 2024," epa.gov, epa.gov/sites/default/files/2019-10/documents/glri-action-plan-3-201910-30pp.pdf.

41. Eurocean, "Cpmr Emphasises Need for Central Role of Regions in 'Future of Europe'," https://www.eurocean.org/, https://www.eurocean.org/np4/255.html.
42. Tavares, *Paradiplomacy: Cities and States as Global Players.*
43. Ibid.
44. Peter Varghese, "Multilateral Challenges in a Federal Context," Australian Government Department of Foreign Affairs and Trade, https://www.dfat.gov.au/news/speeches/Pages/140711_fernberg.
45. Note: the ten provinces are Quebec, Alberta, British Columbia, Manitoba, Newbrunswick, Newfoundland and Labrador, Nova Scotia, Ontario, Prince Edward Island, Saskatchewan.
46. California Department of Finance, "California Becomes World's Sixth Largest Economy," (World Economic Forum, 2017).
47. Mark J. Perry, "Putting America's Ridiculously Large $18t Economy into Perspective by Comparing Us State Gdps to Entire Countries," American Enterprise Institute, https://www.aei.org/publication/putting-americas-ridiculously-large-18t-economy-into-perspective-by-comparing-us-state-gdps-to-entire-countries/.

3

Paradiplomacy: A Global Perspective

From Ancient City-Diplomacy to Paradiplomacy in the 20th century

To trace the origin of paradiplomacy, one needs to delve into the ancient history of mankind when cities and their interaction used to dominate statecraft. In modern times, the study of international relations began with the affairs of nation-states, but the history of the civilisation of the world began with cities. The *Homo sapiens,* known for their predominantly nomadic lifestyle until 10,000 years ago, invented farming and settled down in a community to create societies for harmonious cohabitation. The technological developments and advances in agriculture paved the way for mankind to create civilisations. The concept of urbanisation manifested in the formation of city-states that shaped our political society in the subsequent eras.

The early seeds of civilisation date back to 5000 BC when the Mesopotamian civilisation developed as the first urban civilisation in human history.[1] The Sumerian city-states of Eridu, Bad-tibura, Shuruppak, Uruk, Sippar, Lagash and Kish were formed in the region between the Tigris and Euphrates rivers in the modern-day Middle East.[2] The city of Uruk, being the largest city with a population of 80,000, became a trading centre in 2800 BC. The Sumerian city-states established the earliest form of trade networks across the island of Dilmun (Bahrain), Anatolia (Turkey), Lebanon, Oman and Indus Valley (modern day Pakistan and India).[3] Ancient Egypt was another preeminent civilisation that built cities on the banks of the Nile river in 3000 BC.[4] Cities like Memphis and Thebes remained significant cultural and commercial hubs throughout the period and developed trade partnerships across the Mediterranean region.[5]

The city-states of Mohenjo-Daro and Harappa in South Asia were established in 2500 BC on the banks of the Indus river during the Indus Valley civilisation, also known as the Harappan civilisation (present day Pakistan and Northwest India). Both the cities were well-established urban centres known for their strategic town planning and extensive trade networks among the northern Indus regions. Other urban centres of the Harappan period include Dholavira (India), Ganweriwala (Pakistan) and Rakhigarhi (India). [6]

Further, the Mesoamerican civilisation in North America and the Andean civilisation in South America established many cities to conduct trade and commerce during 1200-1000 BC.[7] The Mesoamerican cities—Chichen Itza, Tikal, Monte Albán or Tenochtitlan—emerged as trading centres that flourished in most of Central America (present day Mexico, Guatemala, Honduras, Belize, El Salvador, Nicaragua and Costa Rica). The Andean civilisation developed commercial and cross- cultural linkages in the Andean regions (present day Venezuela, Colombia, Ecuador, Peru, Bolivia, Chile, and Argentina).[8]

In China, the western Zhou period that began in 1045 BC expanded its economic trade and cultural linkages with various cities that led to the establishment of the earliest trade routes in the cities.[9] In the later period, a historic land route, known as the ancient Silk Road, was established during the Han dynasty in 130 BC that connected the cities of China to the western cities of Rome. Subsequently, the development of land routes and naval routes became a significant form of economic expansion among the western countries in the 16th century.[10]

The ancient city-diplomacy gave utmost importance to trade, commerce and cultural linkages with a mere engagement in political affairs. It was the Roman Empire that institutionalised the idea of city-states during 27 BC. The important trade cities around the Baltic and North Sea were the Hanseatic cities that organised themselves in city leagues, known as the German Hanseatic League, to harmonise their economic, military and diplomatic affairs.[11] The Hanseatic League, within the imperial structure of the Holy Roman Empire, autonomously carried out a collective foreign policy by concluding treaties and developing transnational networks.[12]

The Roman institutions laid the foundation for modern urbanism that became an enduring legacy in European culture. In fact, the Roman empire developed numerous port cities to dominate the Mediterranean Sea and strengthen its maritime trading network. The extensive formation of a road network through city-states allowed the Western Roman Empire (Holy Roman Empire) and Eastern Roman Empire (Byzantine Empire) to control territories in Spain, North Africa and the upper regions of the Middle East until the 15th century, following the conquest of Constantinople (Turkey) by the Ottoman Empire.[13]

Figure 3.1: Ancient Urbanised Cities

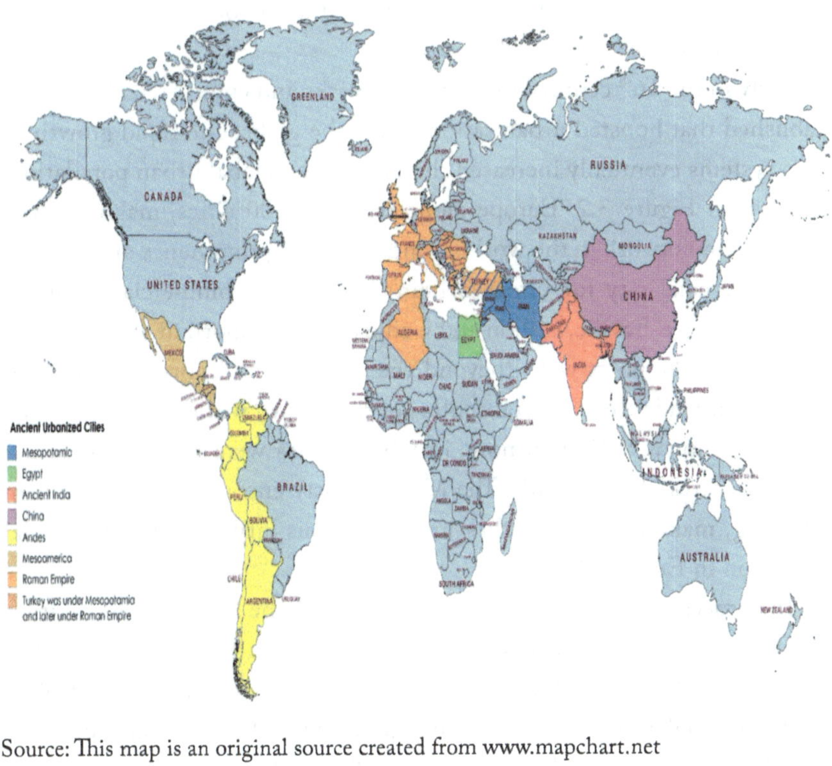

Source: This map is an original source created from www.mapchart.net
The maps are for symbolic purpose, not to scale.

The age of exploration that began in the 15th century set Europe on the path to discover new land routes and sea routes that strengthened the paradiplomatic networks across the globe. The Hanseatic League that consisted of 200 member cities controlled the major inter-city trade and commercial networks and established trading hubs in the cities of Lübeck and Bruges.

The Italian City Republic was another cooperative alliance of cities like Venice and Genoa that dominated the trading activity in the Mediterranean regions.[14] The growing network of European cities denoted an early form of paradiplomacy pertaining to trade, commerce and mining. The European cities expanded their trading and business activities in the Atlantic, following the discovery of America and new sea routes to Asia.[15] In 1498, a Portuguese explorer, Vasco da Gama, established an international trade post in the city of Calicut (Kozhikode) in Kerala (India). Calicut was a crucial link for Europe to develop its maritime trade on the Malabar Coast. Calicut was a widely known international port town of the east-west axis of the emporia trade, connecting Malacca with Venice on the Adriatic Sea.[16]

Early in the 16th century, inter-city networks and commercial hubs were established that boosted urbanisation across the globe. The rapid growth of urban systems eventually increased the flow of the global urban population, as shown in Figure 3.2. Europe alone recorded 500 cities, making it the largest urban network in the world. London gained prominence and became the most crucial city for Great Britain's worldwide commercial empire.[17] Ports like Venice, Seville, Lisbon and Cadiz became important urban centres in Europe. These ports went "beyond their traditional informal hinterland systems that made them pivotal centers of the known world before the mid-sixteenth century."[18] Furthermore, in China, cities were established as the political centres of feudal rule. The Ming dynasty encouraged mercantilism in Beijing, making it the world's most populous city until the Industrial Revolution in Europe.[19]

The process of urbanisation intensified during the Industrial Revolution in the 18th century. For instance, Manchester was a market town with a population of 27,000 until the Industrial Revolution caused an uncontrolled growth of population, increasing it to 95,000, with 52 textile factories in the city.[20] The population in Britain alone was five million in 1700.[21] Industrial cities like London, Liverpool, Manchester and Birmingham attracted businessmen, traders and labourers due to their cross-border connectivity with the urban centres across the continent.[22] England developed an impressive urban network based on its metropolitan dominance in the region.

Figure 3.2: Population from 1500 to 2000

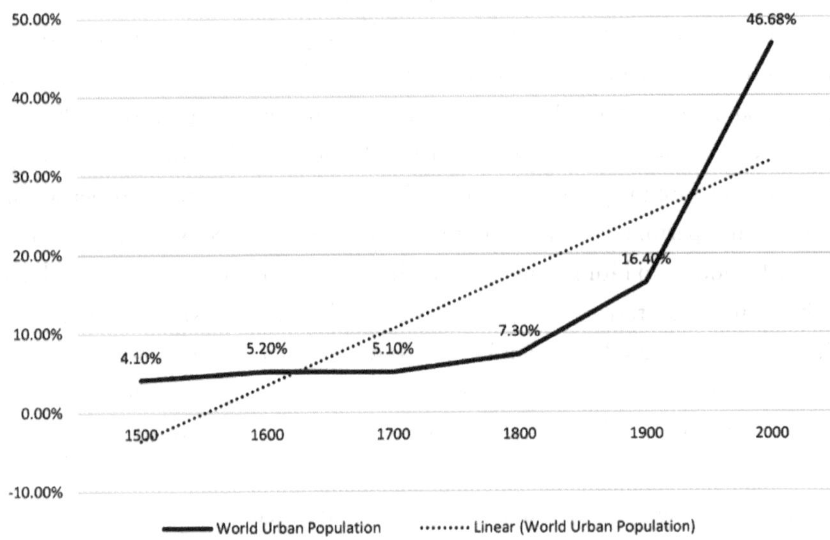

Source: The map is an original source created from data.worldbank.org

The expansion of urban networks and the growth of urban population in the cities boosted the global economy in the 19th century. In the early 1800s, around seven percent of the population lived in cities, which increased to 16 per cent in the 20th century. Due to the mobility of capital, transportation and technology, the distinction between domestic and foreign affairs had eventually been erased/blurred.[23] The cities and subnational governments expanded their global connectivity and laid the groundwork of paradiplomacy. In the late 19th century, the local governments made their first attempts at fostering international exchanges. The crown colonies of Victoria (1857), South Australia (1858), New South Wales (1864), Queensland (1869), Quebec (1882), Tasmania (1886) and Western Australia (1891) under British hegemony appointed their agent-generals to either London or Paris.[24] The province of Quebec appointed its first representative due to a considerable development of financial institutions and enterprises that enhanced the business relations between Quebec and Europe.[25]

In the wake of the 20th century, the cities undertook a paradiplomatic approach to strengthen their foreign interactions and address the global agendas. For instance, in 1907, the state of São Paulo signed its first international agreement with Japanese migration companies to acknowledge the Japanese immigrations into Brazil.[26] The Quebec Ministry of International Relations opened its overseas offices in London (1911) and Brussels (1915).[27] In 1984, Quebec alone operated 22 offices abroad. In Canada, six provinces (Alberta, British Columbia, Nova Scotia, Ontario, Quebec and Saskatchewan) set up 43 offices in foreign political, industrial and financial centres.[28] Alberta, for example, has permanent representatives in Los Angeles, New York, Houston, Tokyo, London and Hong Kong and has further developed special relationships with subnational territorial communities in Japan (the island-province of Hokkaido), the People's Republic of China (province of Heilongjian), and South Korea (province of Gangweon).[29] The US has established 66 permanent overseas offices in 17 countries, of which, 19 are in Tokyo and 11 are in Brussels.[30]

The growing interaction between the cities led to the formation of international organisations and forums. In 1913, the International Union of Local Authorities (IULA) was established in the Netherlands, with an aim to advocate "democratic self-government" among the newly-founded European cities.[31] Post-World War II, European cities concluded town-twinning agreements in 1945 to bring about peace and reconciliation. In 1951, around 50 European mayors formed the Council of European Municipalities, with offices in Austria, Belgium, France, Germany, Great Britain, Ireland, Italy, Luxemburg, the Netherlands, Spain and Switzerland, to establish the standard guidelines for twinning agreements.[32] Later, in 1960, President Eisenhower followed a similar approach, known as sister-city agreements, to develop foreign affairs at the subnational level.[33] In the Soviet Union, the 25th Congress of the Communist Party of the Soviet Union held its first discussion in 1970, where regional leaders expressed an unprecedented interest in foreign affairs.[34]

Until the mid-20th century, the initiatives undertaken by subnational governments were often ad hoc and limited. Subnational activism only gained wide recognition from the international community in the 1980s and 1990s, when the European integration of its subnational entities sparked the economic and political effects of globalisation. The European cities sought new ways to relate to the state, market and the European Union (also known as 'new regionalism'). They were given "constitutional and institutional leeway to develop external activities and could thus adopt a judicially grounded set of instruments for their own diplomatic activities."[35] The 20th century witnessed a period of "Great Divergence" on a global scale, during which the cities were bifurcated based on low-income and high-income regions. "The industrial belt of northern Europe had the highest income region followed by the core regions of North America."[36] North American regions, such as California, emerged as "the first new economy and added the growing city-regions in the Pacific coast to the ranks of the richest large urban regions."[37] The global trade integrated the economies of major industrial cities like Guangzhou (China), Belo Horizonte (Brazil), Bangalore (India), Johannesburg (South Africa) and Kuala Lumpur (Malaysia), to name a few.[38]

According to Tavares, "with the dawn of the new millennium, paradiplomacy has reached its golden age."[39] Until the 20th century, the global visibility of subnational governments could be perceived only in federal countries, such as Canada, Germany, Belgium, Switzerland, Austria and the US and unitary countries like Spain and France. In the 21st century, the practice of paradiplomacy became prominent in the substates of Argentina, Brazil, Chile, China, Japan, India, Mexico, Russia and South Africa.[40] It is an indisputable fact that cities, with their external competencies in economic, political and cultural domains, drove the global agendas and entered into international politics as the emerging paradiplomatic actors of the 21st century.

Global Cities as Paradiplomatic Actors in the 21st century

The 21st century marked the beginning of the urban millennium.[41] Within two centuries, the human species that predominantly lived in rural spaces gradually became urban. The sharp upswing in the urban population since the last century has made us the city-dwelling "Metro-Sapiens."[42] Anna Tibaijuka, the then Executive Director of the UN-Habitat, at the fourth World Urban Forum (2008), held in Nanjing, China, stated that, "The 100 years from 1950 to 2050 will be remembered for the greatest social, cultural, economic and environmental transformation in history—the urbanisation of humanity. With half of us now occupying urban space, the future of the human species is tied to the city."[43] The urban regions became the sole reason behind development and economic globalisation, with cities at the core of the urbanisation process. As rightly said by Michael Storper: "City-regions are the principal scale at which people experience lived reality. The geographical churn, turbulence and unevenness of development, combined with the sheer scale of urbanisation, will make city-region development more important than ever to economics, politics, our global mood and our welfare."[44] According to Tavares, "States and cities are the engines of growth at the ground level, where the transition from policy to practice becomes the most visible."[45]

The analysis made by Price Waterhouse Coopers suggests that, "Urbanisation has been one of the major global themes of the past century and all the indications are that major cities will provide an increasing focus for global economic activity over the course of this century."[46] At the beginning of the 20th century, they were 16 cities with more than one million population in the advanced economic countries. In 2009, as per the UN estimates, the number of cities increased to 400, of which, 300 are found in low and middle-income countries.[47] The UN further predicted that the total global urban population shall increase to five billion by 2030. The UN-Habitat has stated that "More than 75 per cent of the world population will be dwelling in the cities by 2050."[48] These data assert that the cities are becoming the global hubs for economic activities that would further facilitate their paradiplomatic activities in global affairs.

Cities with metropolitan areas are becoming the fulcrum of geo-economics.[49] As per the report of the Chicago Council on Global Affairs (2009), there are 42 cities that contribute to the 100 largest economies in the world.[50] More than half of these cities are in close proximity to a sea coast. The US comprises 12 metropolitan areas, whereas China is home to eight. Around six cities are represented from Western Europe.[51] However, there are no African or Australian cities in the global ranking. Currently, Africa has the least urbanised population, but it has the highest rate of urbanisation. For this reason, the urban population in Africa is estimated to double within 25 years.[52] Moreover, cities contribute an "outsized proportion of their respective national gross domestic product (GDP), accounting for an average economic share that is 1.5 times greater than their share of the national population. For example, Delhi contributes 4 per cent of India's GDP, but is home to less than 2 per cent of the country's population."[53]

The cities with higher engagement in the global economic network and share in the world economy are denoted as 'global cities'. Figure 3.3 provides a comparative study of these global cities based on their GDP from 2008 and their estimated GDP in 2025. The table indicates that the global cities are the potential economic giants in the international political economy. Many cities listed in the table are national political capitals that have greater influence in the country's geoeconomics. There are certain metropolitan areas in the table, which are non-capital cities, whose economic activities have shaped global agendas such as climate governance, irrespective of the international or regional political institutions present within their governing boundaries. This shall be discussed in the following pages.

Figure 3.3: GDP of Top 30 Global Cities 2008-2025

Source: McKinsey Global Institute (2011).

Currently, around 600 urban centers account for about 60 per cent of the global GDP. A study by the Mckinsey Global Institute (2011) has shown that by 2025, around 600 cities will continue to generate the same share of the global GDP.[54] In developed regions, urban areas are the new economic giants. This is discernible from the data that shows that 380 cities in developed regions generated half of the global GDP in 2007, out of which 20 per cent was generated by 190 North American cities. Another 10 per cent came from 220 cities in developing regions. "The middleweight cities are expected to drive 40 per cent of the global growth by 2025, which is more than developed countries and imminent megacities combined."[55, 56] The World Economic Forum predicts that around 15 cities shall become economic and political powerhouses by 2030.[57]

Figure 3.4: Global GDP of Cities by 2030

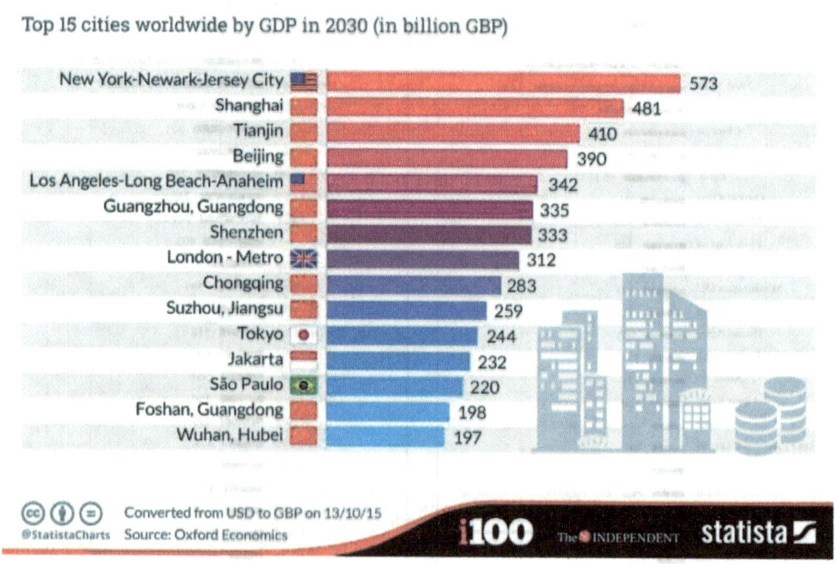

Source: Oxford Economics (2016).

The increasing economic role of cities has caused variations in future growth patterns. For instance, in Asian countries such as China, the emergence of new megacities has fueled its economic growth. In India, urbanisation is still at a preliminary stage, whereas, in Latin America, there is a rapid proliferation of middleweight cities. Therefore, these growth patterns shall not be determined by the 'one size fits all' approach; rather, this requires an extensive study on emerging megacities and middleweight cities as well as their urban markets.

The report by the Chicago Council of Global Affairs suggests that, "Cities' large share of global economic output and their disproportionate share of national GDP could potentially underpin their expanding political influence; as cities expand economically, there is an increase in their participation in policy and governance debates, both nationally and internationally. Yet, for the most part, cities still do not fit into the formal structures of how decisions are made on both national and global issues."[58] However, one cannot deny that sub-states and cities are becoming the paradiplomatic actors in international affairs. The cities are accelerating their international activism across the globe, which has paved a way for mayors, governors and city leaders to exercise their economic and political power in global affairs through effective decision-making. Such paradiplomatic activities have inspired cities as well as states to deal with human scale themes, such as health, education, transportation, culture, terrorism etc. through a 'glocal'[59] perspective.

Figure 3.5: Countries with Global Cities in 21st Century

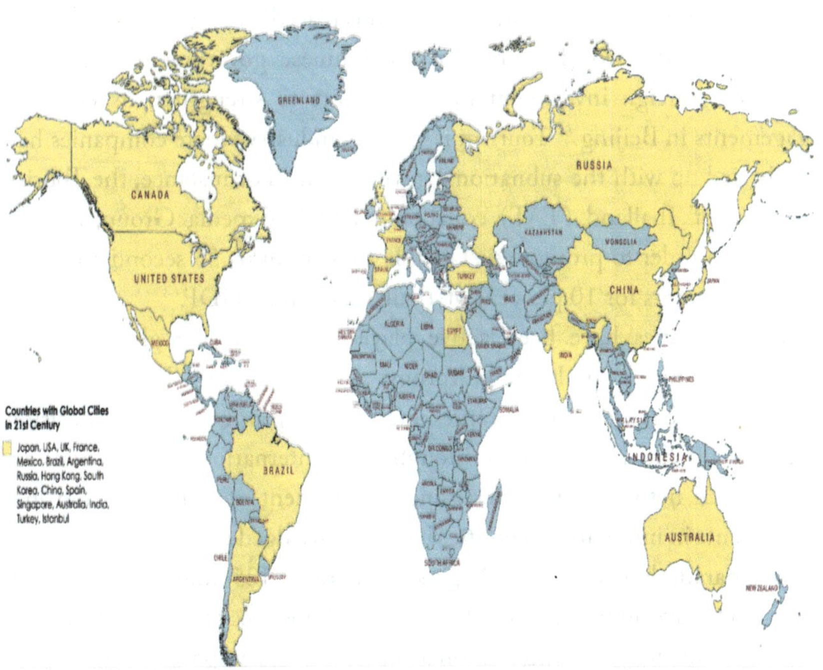

Source: This map is an original source created with www.mapchart.net
The maps are for symbolic purpose, not to scale.

The global economic output of cities and sub-states can be attributed to their increasing economic partnerships through foreign investments from global companies and cultural engagements with foreign cities and subnational entities. For instance, New York City has established a Mayor's Office for International Affairs that focuses on bringing international business to NYC. The programmes conducted by NYC seek industries such as technology and media, smart cities and clean technology, life sciences, fashion and food to attract international investments.[60] Québec is a classic example that has engaged in paradiplomatic affairs with 30 federated states and regions in Western Europe, North America, Africa, Asia and South America. So far, Québec has signed over 776 international agreements, of which 408 are currently in force.[61] São Paulo has 45 sister-city agreements making it the largest ecosystem in South America. The increasing flow of foreign investors and entrepreneurs has resulted in startup development on a large scale.

The Tokyo Metropolitan Government has sister-city agreements with 12 foreign cities.[62] Focused on sports, environment and cultural collaborations. Beijing has tie-ups with 55 sister-cities and is placed among the largest tourist attractions in the world. Currently, the Chinese government is planning to promote foreign investment in new sectors to strengthen its economic engagements in Beijing.[63] Tourism is another industry where companies have directly tied up with the subnational governments. For instance, the Tourism Authority of Thailand (TAT) collaborated with Expedia Group, a global company, in order to promote sustainable tourism in its 55 second-tier cities. Tourism accounts for 10 per cent of Thailand's annual GDP.[64]

Besides, cities have been active players in addressing global agendas by participating in multilateral forums and groupings. The subnational governments that were under-represented in the past became the decision-makers and defined the policies through these international associations and transnational networks. The increasing involvement of municipal and local governments in international politics has acknowledged the role of cities as the evolving paradiplomatic actors. At present, there are 125 multilateral networks where cities have addressed varied issues and challenges at a global level.

The establishment of international bodies has also empowered subnational governments to voice their opinions at a global level. In 1985, the Council of Europe approved the European Charter of Local Self-Government, which stated that "the entitlement of local authorities to belong to an association for the protection and promotion of their common interests and to belong to an international association of local authorities shall be recognised in each State".[65] Further, the establishment of the Committee of Regions (CoR) in 1994 by local and regional representatives of the European Union delegated a significant role to subnational entities in the EU's institutional framework. The European Commission and Council of European Union consults the CoR on legislations based on "economic, social and territorial cohesion, Structural Funds, European Regional Development Fund, European Social Fund, employment and social affairs, education, youth, vocational training, culture and sport, environment, energy and climate change, transport, trans-European networks and public health."[66] The CoR is consulted on 70 per cent of the EU legislations.[67] The Treaty of Lisbon (2007) enhanced the role of the CoR and reshaped the principle of subsidiarity in a way which implies to strengthen the importance of subnational entities. In May 2013, the European Commission communication, "Empowering Local Authorities in Partner Countries for Enhanced Governance and More Effective Development", articulated the European Commission's view on the need to empower local authorities in developing countries around the world. Furthermore, in 2015, the Commission entered into a strategic partnership with five large networks of subnational governments—the AIMF (International Association of Francophones Mayors), CLGF (Commonwealth Local Government Forum), PLATFORMA by CEMR (Council of European Municipalities and Regions) and UCLG (United Cities and Local Governments), marking a new phase in the acknowledgment of local governments in European policy.[68]

Later, various international agencies and bodies were formed with a large participation from local and regional governments in addressing global agendas. In 1992, the UN Conference on Environment and Development in Rio de Janeiro introduced the concept of "Major Groups". "Local Authorities" was one such group. The efforts of subnational and local entities in sustainable development were later recognised in 2012.[69] Furthermore, the United Nations Conferences on Human Settlements (Habitat II) held in Istanbul in 1996 organised its First Assembly of Local Authorities.[70] Later, during Habitat II, a Global Taskforce of Local and Regional Governments was formed to "gather local and regional government leaders and their global organisations in order to build a joint strategy to contribute to the international policy-making debates toward Habitat III."[71] The UN-Habitat strengthened the global presence of cities and subnational governments. In 2000, the United Nations Advisory Committee of Local Authorities was established as a "formal channel to enable local authorities to influence the work programme of the UN-Habitat."[72] The committee is a notable group of "selected mayors and representatives of local authority associations especially chosen on the basis of their local, national and international commitment to engage in the implementation of the Habitat Agenda."[73]

Other UN bodies, such as the UN-DESA, have encouraged paradiplomacy through the Euro- African Partnership for Decentralized Governance, whose aim is "to support decentralisation and decentralised governance in Africa, by means of partnerships between European and African local institutions."[74] The initiative has had minor achievements, but it has been able to carry out some activities for the "promotion of exchange of experiences, information and best practices with regard to decentralisation."[75] Most notably, the Partnership may be credited for shedding light upon the decentralisation efforts in the African countries. Without this platform, these local African initiatives would likely go unnoticed.[76] In 2014, the then UN Secretary-General, Ban Ki-moon, invited "world leaders from government, finance, business and civil society to the Climate Summit 2014 to galvanise and catalyse climate action."[77] The Secretary-General stated that:

> "I ask all Governments to lead and commit to a meaningful, universal climate agreement in Paris in 2015 and to do their fair share to limit global temperature rise to less than 2°C." Outlining the high stakes, he also referred to the "great opportunity" of the climate challenge.[78]

In South America, the Consultative Forum of Cities, States, Provinces and Departments of Mercosur (FCCR) (Advisory Forum of Municipalities, Federated States, Provinces and Departments) was created in 2004 to encourage dialogue and cooperation among local governments. In the foundational document, Mercosur recognised that the development of the integration process has an increasing political dimension, which requires systematic and coordinated actions of the actors involved. Over the years,

FCCR gained institutional density and a fair amount of recognition in the Mercosur countries, but its deliverables are still not impressive, despite the regular meetings of subnational leaders and the vocalisation of ambitions and expectations. This has led the strongest regional economies in the Mercosur space, such as Sao Paulo state, to stay away from the Forum and instead, invest in other international forums.[79]

The global rankings of cities and their economic collaborations suggests that cities have become instrumental in policy-making and driving the global agendas. According to Acuto, "City leaders represent a fundamental bridge between the grand narratives of international affairs and their everyday mundanity."[80] Although cities and states have a prominent place in the global economy, there seems to be insufficient data on their paradiplomatic activities. The scope of paradiplomacy, within the study of international relations, is overlooked by scholars and researchers. Thus, in the global context, the cities have become international players, but are yet to be recognised as paradiplomatic actors. However, climate governance is one exception where cities are playing a discernible global role.

Climate Cities as Global Players

"Cities are on the frontline of the most contemporary global threats, one being climate change."[81] According to the World Economic Forum (WEF), the world's cities are generating more than 75 per cent of the global carbon emissions and this is likely to increase in the future.[82] Cities are already facing challenges of pollution, water scarcity and droughts. Furthermore, 70 per cent of the cities are affected by the sudden onset of disasters and continuing environmental stress ranging from health pandemics to population displacement.[83]

Cities are already facing climate challenges, such as rise in sea level, increasing air pollution, heat stress, mass migration and water scarcity. Air pollution in metropolitan cities like Delhi had reached a hazardous level causing various health problems to urban inhabitants. In Brazil, 850 cities consistently face water scarcity, even though Brazil accounts for 20 per cent of the earth's water reserves. The effects of climate change were visible in Cape Town (South Africa) where water scarcity was called 'Day Zero'—the day when the taps run dry.[84] Being the largest city after Durban in Africa and a top international tourist spot, Cape Town records a population of four million and has declared its water crisis as a national disaster.[85] Cities from the developing world are prone to natural disasters, but lack the financial ability to enhance their infrastructure so as to grapple with natural calamities. Coastal low-lying cities such as Dhaka, Mumbai, Bangkok, Manila and Ho Chi Minh City are highly susceptible to rising sea levels and face the threat of inundation. The city of Jakarta in Indonesia is under the constant threat of floods due to the annual monsoon.[86] A UN report indicates that approximately "400 million urban populations dwell in coastal areas less than 10 metres above sea level and are vulnerable to flooding and storm surges."[87] Nearly 40 per cent of the global population lives in areas less than 100 km from the coast.[88] Out of 20 megacities, around 15 "are at risk from rising sea levels and coastal surges."[89]

Despite the economic well-being of cities and their impressive networking, they still lack soft power to address the urgent global agendas. In addition, nation-states are handicapped in dealing with climate change or reaching an agreement on a multilateral platform. As a result, various cities are at conflict with their respective national governments. One such example is the Paris Climate Accord. After the withdrawal of the United States, more than 100 mayors across the country stepped up by affirming their role in the global agreement, in their effort to fight the climate change at the local level.[90] The mounting political tensions and diverging interests within countries in negotiating international climate policies have convinced cities to assume the centre stage in global climate diplomacy. Hereafter, the notion of city diplomacy gained limelight in curbing climate change at the regional level. Cities augmented their "political influence in national and international arenas by forging inter-city coalitions."[91]

The notion that paradiplomacy was merely confined to town twinning agreements started to change when cities took a global stance in mitigating the environmental challenges through international city networks, such as Cities Climate Leadership Group (C40), Local Governments for Sustainibility (ICLEI) and United Cities and Local Government (UCLG). The Urban LEDS initiative, funded by the European Commission and supported by the ICLEI and the UN-Habitat, aims to expedite the adaptation to "low-emission urban development in emerging economies like India, Brazil, South Africa and Indonesia."[92] The UCLG is an influential network of 1000 cities and 155 national associations that focuses on urban policies and climate agendas.[93] C40 is another global network of 94 megacities, where mayors of cities have collaborated to deliver on "the most ambitious goals of the Paris Agreement at local level."[94] C40 is aimed at "combating climate change and navigating urban action that reduces greenhouse gas emissions and lowers climate risks along with increasing the health, well-being and economic opportunities of urban habitants."[95] C40 currently has "16 networks that cover the mitigation, adaptation and sustainability topics of utmost priority to C40 cities and with the potential for the greatest climate impact."[96]

In 2009, during COP-15, a Climate Summit for Mayors was organised for the first time to discuss the issue. The Summit for Mayors was jointly organised by the city of Copenhagen, C40 and ICLEI.[97] The summit was attended by nearly 500 delegates and 79 cities participated with 67 mayors and deputy mayors.[98] Later, the Mayors' Task Force on Climate Change and the Urban Poor was founded by the mayors of Dar es Salaam, Jakarta, Mexico City and Sao Paulo.[99] The Intergovernmental Panel on Climate Change (IPCC) further dedicated its first chapter to the issues of human settlement and cities.[100] Currently, around 200 intercity networks are working with each other to combat issues ranging from migration to climate change. "More than 8,000 cities have introduced solar power, while 300 cities are completely energy autonomous, some even exporting power back into national grids."[101]

Since 2018, the inter-city network has empowered "more than 9,100 cities representing 780 million people to agree on a global pact to meet and ideally exceed the Paris Climate Agreement targets."[102] "Because of the sheer volume of economic activity and concentrated resource usage over which they have at least some degree of jurisdiction, cities are well-positioned to pursue agendas of urban metabolic efficiency and generate meaningful impact independent of nation-states."[103] A project named "The New Climate Economy" has explained "how urban density and compact cities can lower the carbon footprint."[104, 105] If cities learn to reduce their carbon footprints, it can pave the way for all towards a sustainable future. Through participation in transnational municipal networks such as C40, "cities can multiply their impact not only by sharing best practices, but also by consolidating their leverage as advocates for climate action."[106]

"Climate change has added a layer of urgency and complexity to an already crowded agenda."[107] In 2010, the World Bank published a report, "Cities and Climate Change: An Urgent Agenda" that is centered on three issues dealing with climate change—"How cities contribute to and are affected by climate change; how policy makers can use cities to change human behaviour and improve technology related to climate change; and how cities should use climate change as an opportunity to raise their profile, reinforce sensible policies and move toward a more sustainable community and planet."[108] A report on "Cities and Climate Diplomacy" points out that "cities practice climate diplomacy through four different mechanisms: (i) networks; (ii) bilateral relations with other cities; (iii) local-national city relations and (iv) city-global multilateral mechanisms. The last mechanism is not an option for most cities and only applies to city-states (e.g. Singapore) that have direct representation and a diplomatic role in global climate governance regimes, which includes the UN Framework Convention on Climate Change (UNFCCC) and the UN Conference on Sustainable Development (UNCSD)."[109]

Climate diplomacy can only prevail between two cities when they seek mutual benefits in their relationship. Most bilateral diplomacy exists between cities whose either stages of economic development or implementation capacities are different from each other. In such cases, "one serves as a resource city, seeking recognition, while the other city serves as a recipient or experimental city, seeking models or best practices to tailor to its own local context."[110] For instance, city-to-city cooperation between Bangkok and Yokohama on sustainable urban development indicates that initiatives like Yokohama's Partnership of Resources and Technologies (Y-PORT) sets out "as a brand that can promote Yokohama's environmental technologies which other cities can resort to."[111]

Most of the government planning agencies, such as the World Bank, international finance institutions, private sector partners and think tanks have incorporated climate change and urbanisation into their strategies. The client cities of the World Bank run a financial aid programme and provide analytical services on a large scale compared to most of the countries. Cairo, Jakarta, Mexico City and Sao Paulo have formed partnerships with the World Bank to develop comprehensive assistance programmes that are equivalent/comparable to those of other countries.[112] The World Bank and its key partners, such as the UNEP, UN-HABITAT and Cities Alliance, provide an array of tools to policy makers, city managers and urban researchers. Some of the ongoing tools are enlisted below:[103]

i. **Global City Indicators Programme:** The World Bank and its key partners launched this programme at the 4th Urban Forum in Nanjing (China). The programme has established a "set of city indicators with a global standardised methodology that allows global comparability of city performance and knowledge-sharing."[104]
ii. **Greenhouse Gas Emission Standards:** The UNEP and UN-Habitat have inaugurated a "harmonised protocol for quantifying city GHG emissions with a standardised means of measurement." This would provide a regular update on the large cities that will further foster city inventories.[105]
iii. **The Energy Sector Management Assistance Programme:** The ESMAP is managed by the World Bank and provides a technical assistance partnership and imparts global knowledge. In 2008, the Energy Efficient Cities Initiative (EECI) was launched by the ESMAP to assist cities in meeting their energy challenges. The EECI is a "flexible and demand-driven programme that identifies innovative ways to improve energy efficiency in the delivery of city services and reduce the costs and environmental impacts of energy use."[106]

These are a few instances that indicate the strong representation of cities in international forums and programmes. It is an indisputable fact that climate change is one such agenda where cities and subnational entities have exerted their influence within a global perspective (for example, C40). While countries were attempting to arbitrate the international climate policies, subnational actors stepped up to establish their paradiplomatic role in mitigating climate changes. As mentioned above, the initiatives undertaken by cities to curb environmental problems extended the scope of paradiplomatic affairs. Apart from addressing global challenges, cities have also strengthened their presence in the international economy. From developing cultural linkages by following ancient city-diplomacy to promoting economic interactions through paradiplomacy, cities and subnational governments collectively engaged to vanguard the global environmental challenges.

This chapter studied the early form of paradiplomacy that prevailed among the ancient cities and included a short narrative on the paradiplomacy practiced by modern cities in the 20th century. The notion of paradiplomacy gained a strong foothold in the early 20th century and deepened its practices in the 21st century. The chapter concludes that paradiplomacy is not an unprecedented concept; rather, it is one that evolved over centuries. The practices of paradiplomacy in the economic, cultural and environmental domains gained limelight in the 21st century that defined its global trend. The chapter also explored how economic integration due to globalisation has pervaded the practice of paradiplomacy among many of the federal countries. Besides, the growing global engagement of the cities suggests that paradiplomacy will emerge as a global phenomenon and determine the foreign policies of nations in the foreseeable future.

Notes

1. Joshua J. Mark, "Sumer," World History Encyclopedia, https://www.worldhistory.org/sumer/.
2. The Editors of Encyclopaedia, "Sumer," Britannica, https://www.britannica.com/place/Sumer.
3. Evan Andrews, "9 Things You May Not Know About the Ancient Sumerians," www.history.com, https://www.history.com/news/9-things-you-may-not-know-about-the-ancient-sumerians.
4. Joshua J. Mark, "Ancient Egypt," World History Encyclopedia, https://www.worldhistory.org/egypt/.
5. Ibid.
6. Harappa.com, "Major Sites and Interaction Networks", www.harappa.com, https://www.harappa.com/indus2/161.html.
7. Pamela Crossley Richard Bulliet, Daniel Headrick, Steven Hirsch, Lyman Johnson, *The Earth and Its Peoples: A Global History*, Peoples and Civilizations of the Americas, 200-1500 (Boston: Houghton Mifflin, 2008).
8. Ibid.
9. Joshua J. Mark, "Zhou Dynasty," World History Encyclopedia.
10. Richard Bulliet, *The Earth and Its Peoples: A Global History*.
11. Janne E. Nijman, "Renaissance of the City as Global Actor. The Role of Foreign Policy and International Law Practices in the Construction of Cities as Global Actors," *T.M.C. Asser Institute for International & European Law* 2 (2016).
12. Ibid.

13. National Geographic, "Roman Empire: Road and Trade Network," nationalgeogrophic.org, https://www.nationalgeographic.org/media/roman-empire-road-and-trade-network/.
14. Diercke International Atlas, "Trade and Economy in the 15th Century," http://www.diercke.com/, http://www.diercke.com/kartenansicht.xtp?artId=978-3-14-100790-9&stichwort=slave&fs=1.
15. Ibid.
16. K.S Mathew, "Calicut, the International Emporium of Maritime Trade and the Portuguese During the Sixteenth Century," *Proceedings of the Indian History Congress* 67 (2006).
17. Donald J. Harreld, "Merchants and International Trade Networks in the Sixteenth Century," *XIV International Economic History Congress, Helsinki* (2006).
18. Cátia Antunes, "Early Modern Ports, 1500–1750," EGO, http://ieg-ego.eu/en/threads/crossroads/courts-and-cities/catia-antunes-early-modern-ports-1500-1750.
19. Timothy Brook, "The Merchant Network in 16th Century China: A Discussion and Translation of Zhang Han's "on Merchants"," *Journal of the Economic and Social History of the Orient, BRILL* 24, no. 2 (1981).
20. Matthew White, "The Rise of Cities in the 18th Century," https://www.bl.uk/georgian-britain/articles/the-rise-of-cities-in-the-18th-century.
21. Ibid.
22. Hannah Brown, "Uk Cities in the Global Economy," https://www.centreforcities.org/, https://www.centreforcities.org/wp-content/uploads/2014/09/08-09-09-UK-cities-in-the-global-economy.pdf.
23. Tavares, *Paradiplomacy: Cities and States as Global Players*, p.10.
24. Ibid., p. 11.
25. Ibid.
26 Junichi Goto, "Latin Americans of Japanese Origin (Nikkeijin) Working in Japan—a Survey", ed. World Bank Policy Research Working Paper (World Bank 2007).
27. Tavares, *Paradiplomacy: Cities and States as Global Players.*
28. Duchacek, "The International Dimension of Subnational Self-Government."
29. Ibid.
30. Ibid.
31. Tavares, *Paradiplomacy: Cities and States as Global Players.*
32. CEMR, "Introducing Cemr," European section of United Cities and Local Governments, https://www.ccre.org/en/article/introducing_cemr.
33. centerforcitizendiplomacy.org, "Sister Cities International," www.centerforcitizendiplomacy.org, https://www.centerforcitizendiplomacy.org/network/sister-cities-international/.

34. Tavares, *Paradiplomacy: Cities and States as Global Players*, p. 13.
35. Ibid., p. 14.
36. Michael Storper, "Cities and Region in the Twenty-First Century: Why Do They Develop and Change," in *Keys to the City: How Economics, Institution, Social Interactions and Politics Shape the Development* (New Jersey: Princeton University Press, 2013).
37. Ibid.
38. Ibid.
39. Tavares, *Paradiplomacy: Cities and States as Global Players*, p. 14.
40. Ibid.
41. UN, "World Entering 'Urban Millennium', Secretary-General Tells Opening Meeting of Habitat Special Session," news release, 2001, https://www.un.org/press/en/2001/GA9867.doc.htm.
42. Jason Vargo, "Metro Sapiens: An Urban Species," *Journal of Environmental Studies and Sciences volume* 4 (2014).
43. Tavares, *Paradiplomacy: Cities and States as Global Players.*
44. "Harmonious Urbanization: The Challenge of Balanced Territorial Development," in *The fourth session of the World Urban Forum* (Nanjing, China: UN Habitat, 2008).
45. *Paradiplomacy: Cities and States as Global Players*, p. 5.
47. "Global City Gdp Rankings 2008-2025," *Price Waterhouse Cooper Economic Outlook* (2009), http://pwc.blogs.com/files/global-city-gdp-rankings-2008-2025.pdf.
47. As per 2018, low-income economies are defined as those with a GNI per capita of $1,005 or less in 2016; lower middle-income economies are those with a GNI per capita between $1,006 and $3,955; upper middle-income economies are those with a GNI per capita between $3,956 and $12,235; high-income economies are those with a GNI per capita of $12,236 or more. *Retrieved from* https://datahelpdesk.worldbank.org/knowledgebase/articles/906519-world-bank-country-and-lending-groups
48. "Harmonious Urbanization: The Challenge of Balanced Territorial Development."
49. Geoeconomics is the study of the spatial, temporal and political aspects of economies and resources.
50. Sam Tabory Noah Toly, "100 Top Economies: Urban Influence and the Position of Cities in an Evolving World Order," in *Global Cities* (US: Chicago Council on Global Affairs, 2016).
51. Ibid.
52. CSIS, "Urbanization in Sub-Saharan Africa," https://www.csis.org/, https://www.csis.org/analysis/urbanization-sub-saharan-africa.
53. Noah Toly, "100 Top Economies: Urban Influence and the Position of Cities in an Evolving World Order."

54. Richard Dobbs et al., "Urban World: Mapping the Economic Power of Cities," (Mckinsey Global Institute, 2011).
55. Megacities are defined as metropolitan areas with ten million or more inhabitants. Middleweights are cities with populations of between 150,000 and ten million inhabitants.
56. Richard Dobbs et al., "Urban World: Mapping the Economic Power of Cities."
57. Tavares, "Forget the Nation-State: Cities Will Transform the Way We Conduct Foreign Affairs".
58. Noah Toly, "100 Top Economies: Urban Influence and the Position of Cities in an Evolving World Order."
59. The word 'glocal' is an approach that connects local agendas with global affairs
60. NYC.gov, "Economic Development," Mayor's Office for International Affairs, https://www1.nyc.gov/site/international/services/international-business.page.
61. mrif.gouv.qc.ca, "Ministère Des Relations Internationales Et De La Francophonie," Government of Québec, http://www.mrif.gouv.qc.ca/en/Ententes-et-Engagements/Ententes-internationales.
62. seisakukikaku.metro.tokyo.lg.jp, "Tokyo's City Diplomacy,"Tokyo Metropolitan Government, https://www.seisakukikaku.metro.tokyo.lg.jp/en/diplomacy/city-to-city-diplomacy/agreement.html.
63. ebeijing.gov.cn, "Sister Cities of Beijing," http://www.ebeijing.gov.cn/Sister_Cities_2017/.
64. TATNEWS.org, "Tourism Authority of Thailand and Expedia Group Announce a Memorandum of Understanding," news release, 2018, https://www.tatnews.org/2018/09/tourism-authority-of-thailand-and-expedia-group-announce-a-memorandum-of-understanding/.
65. Tavares, *Paradiplomacy: Cities and States as Global Players*, p. 55.
66. EUROPA, "The Eu's Assembly of Regional and Local Representatives," European Committee of the Regions, https://cor.europa.eu/en/about/Pages/default.aspx.
67. Ibid.
68. Tavares, *Paradiplomacy: Cities and States as Global Players*, p. 55.
69. Ibid., p. 56.
70. UN, "Report of the United Nations Conference on Human Settlements (Habitat Ii)," https://www.un.org/, https://www.un.org/ruleoflaw/wp-content/uploads/2015/10/istanbul-declaration.pdf.
71. Tavares, *Paradiplomacy: Cities and States as Global Players*, p. 57.
72. UN, "The United Nations Advisory Committee of Local Authorities (Unacla)," https://mirror.unhabitat.org/, https://mirror.unhabitat.org/content.asp?cid=89&catid=366&typeid=24&subMenuId=0.
73. Ibid.

74. Tavares, *Paradiplomacy: Cities and States as Global Players.*
75. Ibid.
76. Ibid., p. 57.
77. UN, "As World Leaders Come Together for Historic Climate Summit, Secretary-General Urges Commitment to Meaningful, Universal Agreement," news release, 2014, https://www.un.org/press/en/2014/envdev1457.doc.htm.
78. Ibid.
79. Tavares, *Paradiplomacy: Cities and States as Global Players*, p. 58.
80. Ibid., p. 28.
81. Robert Muggah, "Cities Are on the Front-Line of Climate Change. They Must Adapt or Die," World Economic Forum, https://www.weforum.org/agenda/2016/10/cities-are-on-the-front-line-of-climate-change-they-must-adapt-or-die/.
82. Oliver Cann, "Time for Cities to Step up to the Challenge of Climate Change," World Economic Forum, https://www.weforum.org/press/2017/11/time-for-cities-to-step-up-to-the-challenge-of-climate-change.
83. Muggah, "Cities Are on the Front-Line of Climate Change. They Must Adapt or Die".
84. Ed Stoddard; Victor Antonie, "South Africa's Water Crisis Spreads from Cape Town," Reuters, https://www.reuters.com/article/us-safrica-drought-lesotho/south-africas-water-crisis-spreads-from-cape-town-idUSKBN1FK27A.
85. Ibid.
86. John Rennie Short, "How Cities Are Adapting to Climate Change," World Economic Forum, https://www.weforum.org/agenda/2015/07/how-cities-are-adapting-to-climate-change/.
87. UN, "Report on the Ocean Conference," https://www.un.org/, https://www.un.org/sustainabledevelopment/wp-content/uploads/2017/05/Ocean-fact-sheet-package.pdf.
88. Ibid.
89. worldbank.org, "Cities and Climate Change: An Urgent Agenda," in *Urban Development Series Knowledge Papers* (Washington D.C: The International Bank for Reconstruction and Development/The World Bank, 2010), p. 16.
90. Penny Abeywardena, "To Tackle Climate Change, We Need City Diplomacy," World Economic Forum, https://www.weforum.org/agenda/2018/05/to-tackle-climate-change-we-need-city-diplomacy-greenland-new-york/.
91. Robert Muggah, "How Cities, Not States, Can Solve the World's Biggest Problems," World Economic Forum, https://www.weforum.org/agenda/2018/10/how-cities-not-states-can-solve-the-world-s-biggest-problems/.
92. Kaj Fischer et al., "Urbanization and Climate Diplomacy," in *The Stake of Cities in Global Climate Governance* (Federal Foreign Office: Adelphi, 2015), p. 9.

93. Ibid., p. 7.
94. "C40 Cities Climate Leadership Group".
95. Ibid.
96. Ibid.
97. COE, "18th Plenary Session of the Congress," Council of Europe, https://rm.coe.int/168071a5b9.
98. worldbank.org, "Cities and Climate Change: An Urgent Agenda."
99. Abha Joshi-Ghani, "Learning to Leverage Climate Action in Cities," worldbank.org, https://blogs.worldbank.org/sustainablecities/learning-leverage-climate-action-cities.
100. worldbank.org, "Cities and Climate Change: An Urgent Agenda."
101. Cann, "Time for Cities to Step up to the Challenge of Climate Change."
102. Muggah, "How Cities, Not States, Can Solve the World's Biggest Problems."
103. Noah Toly, "100 Top Economies: Urban Influence and the Position of Cities in an Evolving World Order."
104. Muggah, "Cities Are on the Front-Line of Climate Change. They Must Adapt or Die."
105. Carbon footprint is the amount of carbondioxide released into the atmosphere as a result of the activities of a particular individual, organisation, or community.
106. Noah Toly, "100 Top Economies: Urban Influence and the Position of Cities in an Evolving World Order."
107. worldbank.org, "Cities and Climate Change: An Urgent Agenda."
108. Ibid.
109. Gianna Gayle Herrera Amul and Maxim Shrestha, "Cities and Climate Diplomacy in Asia Pacific," *Climate Diplomacy* (2015), www.climate-diplomacy.org
110. Ibid., p. 3.
111. Ibid.
112. worldbank.org, "Cities and Climate Change: An Urgent Agenda," p. 40.
113. Ibid., p. 41.
114. Ibid.
115. Ibid.
116. Ibid.

4

Paradiplomacy and India

Paradiplomacy, which was a widely prevalent phenomenon in the 20th century, became visible in India's foreign policy only in the initial years of the 21st century. In this chapter, an in-depth study is attempted on the involvement of Indian states and cities in foreign policy undertakings. The influence of Indian states was minimal in the early post-independence phase, but it gradually increased in 1991, largely due to the economic reforms. The chapter examines how the increasing practice of paradiplomacy in foreign policy conduct has defined India's economic growth trajectory and infrastructure development. The chapter brings to fore, the role of Indian states in practicing paradiplomacy, which is mainly confined to economic cooperation.

This chapter suggests paradiplomacy as being an economic compulsion rather than a diplomatic offshoot. The chapter traces the paradiplomatic initiatives in the pre-reform period (1947-1990) when the foreign interaction of Indian states and cities was minimal, probably due to the extremely centralised polity and statecraft in India. Another chapter focuses on the post-reform period (1990-present day) and analyses the onset of economic liberalisation in India and how it paved the way for paradiplomacy in the country. With the opening up of the Indian economy, Indian states have become ideal destinations for foreign investment and economic tie-ups through 'sister-cities'[1] and 'twinning' agreements.[2]

Both chapters attempt to examine how the practice of paradiplomacy strengthened India's economic growth and its global economic participation. In addition, state governments' own initiatives help one to understand the future of paradiplomacy in India and its importance in foreign policy. The chapters attempt to uncover the journey of the Indian states and cities from being passive observers to becoming potential paradiplomatic actors in India's foreign policy.

Pre-Reform Period (1947-1990)

The Indian political scene in the post-independence phase was dominated by the Indian National Congress (INC) party at the state level as well as at the centre. Till 1967, the Congress party emphasised on a highly centralised political structure. The Fourth General Elections held in 1967 resulted in the end of the Congress' single party majority rule and the onset of coalition politics in India in several states. But in 1980, the Congress party, led by Indira Gandhi, reestablished its power in the centre and in several states during the mid-term elections of the Lok Sabha. "The 42nd Amendment Act (1976) had also increased the powers of the central government at the expense of the states."[3]

Theorist K.C Wheare has characterised the Indian Constitution as quasi-federal in nature—a unitary state with federal features.[4] Under the Article 246 of the Indian Constitution, the legislative powers are divided into three lists—the State List, Union List and Concurrent List.[5] As per the Union List, the Union government alone can make the laws on almost all matters related to foreign policy, treaties, interstate trade agreements, defence and security. Under the Nehruvian foreign policy model,[6] the role of the states was quite negligible in foreign policy matters and decision-making process. Moreover, the participation of the states and cities in the conduct of India's foreign policy during the pre-reform period (1947-1990) was not only limited, but also mostly not recorded. Very few documents are available on the agreements and partnerships between the cities to identify the early practice of paradiplomacy in India during this period. Till 1990, most of the states and cities in India mainly engaged in cultural exchanges through sister-city and twinning agreements.

The Early Instances of Paradiplomacy

The earliest known practice of paradiplomacy dates back to 1963, when Mumbai (then Bombay) signed its sister-city agreement with St. Petersburg (then Leningrad under the USSR).[7] "Given the traditional and long-lasting political, economic, commercial and cultural ties with Russia, St. Petersburg became the first sister-city of Mumbai in 1967."[8] In December 2004, during President Putin's visit to India, an agreement on cooperation was signed.[9] Both the coastal cities held a celebration of the 50th anniversary of this agreement in 2017, which was attended by dignitaries from St. Petersburg and the former Mayor of Mumbai, V. Mahadeshwar.[10] Back in 1966, Chennai, then known as Madras, formed its first sister-city relationship with Volgograd (Russia) through a special agreement to enhance its cultural ties with the city.[11]

In 1968, Mangalore entered a twinning agreement with Hamilton (Canada).[12] In the same year, Bombay (Mumbai) became a sister-city of Stuttgart (Germany), with an objective of 'City Partnership', to encourage "friendly contacts, respect, mutual understanding and lasting friendship between the inhabitants of the two cities."[13] Mumbai also established a sister-city relationship with Honolulu (Hawaii) in 1970[14] and another with Los Angeles (USA) in 1972.[15] Furthermore, in 1973, Bangalore concluded a twinning agreement with Minsk (Belarus).[16] In Minsk, a square that, until 1986, was named after Maxim Gorky, was renamed as the 'Bangalore Square' in order to foster this friendship. In turn, Bangalore named one of its squares, the 'Minsk Square', in honour of the capital of Belarus.[17] Similarly, the Bremen Chowk in Pune was so named because of the city friendship that was established in 1976 between Pune and Bremen (Germany).[18] The focus of this friendship was primarily on development and economic cooperation. Later, a MoU was signed in 1998 to enhance the partnership between the cities.

In 1982, Manipal became the twin city of Loma Linda (California), in a ceremony under the auspices of the Sister Cities International.[19] Furthermore, Chennai established friendship with Denver (USA) and joined the Denver Sister Cities International (DSCI) in 1984 to "promote cultural, educational and humanitarian initiatives, along with student/community exchanges, lectures and various cultural gatherings."[20] The sister-city agreement between San Jose, California and Pune was proposed in 1989,[21] which was implemented in 1992 and the cities have continued their cultural partnership since then.[22]

Figure 4.1: Sister-cities Agreement during the Pre-Reform Period (1947-1990)

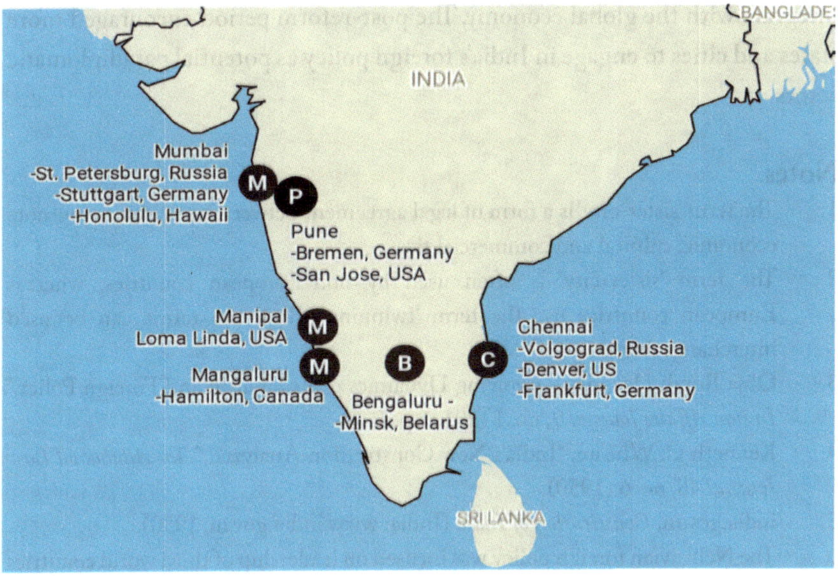

Source: This map is an original source created with app.datawrapper.de
The maps are for symbolic purpose, not to scale.

These notable instances indicate that most of these twinning agreements and sister-city relationships were concluded due to many similarities between the cities in terms of size and population. These cities have built strong partnerships through common interests, such as education, cultural ties, economic cooperation, infrastructure development, sustainable environment and global connectivity. One of the challenges in studying these practices of paradiplomacy in the pre-reform period is the limitation of data on such developments. There are many sister-city agreements and city partnerships which were not documented during that time. Besides, the agreements that were documented lack details on how these agreements were implemented by the cities and whether they were renewed in the following years. For instance, Madras (Chennai) entered into a sister-city agreement with Frankfurt (Germany), but there are no records to substantiate the timeline of this agreement.[23]

Besides, the sister-city and twinning agreements were mainly concluded by the central government due to the constitutional provisions that limited the participation of the Indian states and cities in external affairs. However, this changed in 1990, when India set out to liberalise its economy in order to integrate with the global economy. The post-reform period encouraged more states and cities to engage in India's foreign policy as potential paradiplomatic actors.

Notes

1. The term 'sister-city' is a form of legal agreement between two cities to promote economic, cultural and commercial ties.
2. The term 'sister-city' is often used by non-European countries; whereas European countries use the term 'twinning'. Both the terms can be used interchangeably.
3. Obja Borah Hazarika, "Evolving Dynamics of Federalism and Foreign Policy," *Indian Affairs Journal* 9, no. 1 (2014), p. 5.
4. Kenneth C. Wheare, "India's New Constitution Analyzed," *The Allahabad Law Journal* 48, no. 6 (1950).
5. india.gov.in, *Constitution of India* (India: www.india.gov.in, 1950).
6. The Nehruvian foreign policy was focused on leadership of third world countries through Non-Aligned Movement, Panchsheel or the five principles of peaceful co-existence and improving bilateral relations with Pakistan after the partition.
7. cgispburg.gov.in, "St. Petersburg: Fact Sheet," news release, https://cgispburg.gov.in/useful-information-about-spb.php.
8. "India and North-West Federal Region of Russia," news release, https://cgispburg.gov.in/india-and-north-west-region-of-russian-federation.php.
9. Ibid.
10. ind-mum.rs.gov.ru, "Gala Concert at the Royal Opera House, Mumbai to Celebrate the 50th Anniversary of Sister Cities with St. Petersburg," news release, https://ind-mum.rs.gov.ru/en/news/21880.
11. facebook.com, "Embassy of India in Moscow," Official Page, https://www.facebook.com/IndiaInRussia/posts/chennai-and-volgograd-became-sister-cities-back-in-1966-they-signed-a-special-ag/3361291893913599/.
12. mundalization.ca, "Twinning," https://www.mundialization.ca/activities/twinning/.
13. cgimunich.gov.in, "Indo-Baden Wurttemberg Relations," cgimunich.gov.in, https://cgimunich.gov.in/pages.php?id=12618.
14. www.honolulu.gov, "International/Sister Cities," City and County of Honolulu, https://www.honolulu.gov/ecodev/intl-relations/194-site-may-oed-cat/28493-city-of-mumbai.html.
15. sistercitiesofla.org, "Our Sister Cities," https://sistercitiesofla.org/sister-cities/mumbai/.

16. minskherald.com, "Bangalore's Tales of Minsk Square," The Minsk Herald http://minskherald.com/2016/01/bangalores-tales-of-minsk-square/.
17. Agentika, "Bangalore Square," agentika.com, https://agentika.com/ru/encyclopedia/b1dc3f68-6f4e-4297-9cb9-535196800a7f/places/root/1a93d13d-01af-488d-9edc-61d76a08c2f8?version=Uwo-0.
18. india.diplo.de, "City-Friendship between Bremen and Pune," German Missions in India, https://india.diplo.de/in-de/vertretungen/gkmumbai/bremen-pune/2066692.
19. lomalinda-ca.gov, "Sister Cities", https://www.lomalinda-ca.gov/our_city/sister_cities.
20. www.denvergov.org, "Denver Sister Cities International", Human Rights and Community Partnerships, https://www.denvergov.org/content/denvergov/en/human-rights-and-community-partnerships/programs---initiatives/denver-sister-cities.html.
21. sanjosepunesistercity.org, "Stimulate Interaction between People of San Jose (Us) and Pune (India)."
22. www.grpg.org, "Sister City Seating Areas", https://www.grpg.org/, https://www.grpg.org/sister-city-seating-areas/#:~:text=Pun%C3%A9%2C%20India&text=San%20Jose%20and%20Pune%20established,on%20a%20cultural%20partnership%20since.
23. chennaimadras.blogspot.com, "Sister Act", http://chennaimadras.blogspot.com/, http://chennaimadras.blogspot.com/2008/09/sister-act.html.

5

Paradiplomacy in India in the Post-Reform Period

The onset of the coalition era in Indian politics in 1967 and the liberalisation of the Indian economy in 1990 are the two key factors that created conditions for Indian states and cities to play a role in foreign policy. The need for decentralisation in the "form of an increased sharing of decision-making in India was voiced by various regional parties in 1983 and the Sarkaria Commission was established to study the state of federal relations in India."[1] In 1989, the growing participation of the regional parties in federal governance led to the beginning of coalition politics in India. Simultaneously, the economic reforms of 1991 opened the doors for Indian chief ministers to invite foreign investments for their respective states.

Specifically, paradiplomacy gained momentum in India in 1993, when a power purchase agreement was concluded by the Maharashtra State Electricity Board with the Dabhol Power Company (DPC). This was a joint venture between three US-based multinational corporations—Enron, General Electrical Corporation and Bechtel Enterprises Incorporated.[2] For the first time, a state solely engaged in a diplomatic negotiation for a single largest foreign direct investment (FDI) in India and the central government played a supportive role in it. Eventually, other Indian states followed in its wake that led to the opening up of the Indian economy. The New Economic Policy of 1991 introduced by the then prime minister, P.V. Narasimha Rao and the then finance minister, Dr. Manmohan Singh, reduced the governmental control on the industrial sector. This further provided opportunities to the state governments to seek their own development strategies. Eventually, the states pursued foreign investments without "routing their efforts through the central bureaucracy."[3] Moreover, the states started to take interest in and exercise considerable influence over foreign policy matters. "The West Bengal Chief Minister, Jyoti Basu, during the United Front government's term in office (1977-2000), played a vital role in the resolution of the Ganges water conflict between India and Bangladesh. In December 1996, during his official visit to Bangladesh, he held negotiations and preceded a water sharing treaty for both the countries (held negotiations that paved the way for a water-sharing treaty between both the countries)."[4]

In 1999, the economic liberalisation process coincided with the multi-party coalition government in India. The emergence of a coalition government formed by the National Democratic Alliance, Janata Dal, Janata Party and United Progressive Alliance I and II, gave considerable leverage to the states governed by these member parties in the union government's policies.[5] The end of single-party rule followed by the beginning of coalition politics facilitated greater involvement of the states and cities in the diplomatic affairs of India. For instance, the former chief minister of Andhra Pradesh, Chandrababu Naidu, concluded MoUs to attract "investments on matters ranging from agriculture, IT, education and sports to development grants." Naidu was also the first to negotiate a state-level World Bank development loan for a constituent unit in India."[6] The then chief minister of Gujarat, Narendra Modi, introduced 'Vibrant Gujarat'[7] in 2003, which made Gujarat an ideal destination for foreign investments. In 2007, during the Vibrant Gujarat Investor's Summit, "around 343 MoUs worth 4,61,835 crores were signed with foreign companies."[8] In 2009, "8668 MoUs with a total investment of 12,24,482 crores were formalised. The number further increased in 2011, when nearly 8,000 MoUs worth $450 billion were made official."[9] After Narendra Modi became the prime minister, the term 'paradiplomacy' has been widely used to highlight the indispensable role played by the states in the conduct of India's foreign policy. The practice of paradiplomacy became a prominent subject of foreign policy debate when Prime Minister Narendra Modi called for "greater role for states in India's economic diplomacy."[10] In his inaugural address at the Delhi Economics Conclave in November 2015, Modi stated that:

> In a break with over 65 years of tradition, we have involved states even in foreign policy. The Ministry of External Affairs has been asked to work with the states. When I visited China, a state-to-state summit was also held. And states have been asked to create export promotion councils. Making the states think globally is yet another reform with potential to transform.[11]"

The 2017 report of the Reserve Bank of India stated that in the last 17 years, six Indian states, i.e., Andhra Pradesh, Gujarat, Karnataka, Maharashtra, New Delhi and Tamil Nadu accounted for over 70 per cent of the FDI equity flows to India. Maharashtra and Delhi generated over 50 per cent of FDI flows during this period. Maharashtra alone accounted for over 30 per cent of FDI inflows during this period.[12] In 2020, Maharashtra was replaced by Gujarat, which accounted for 35 per cent of FDI inflows, whereas Maharashtra accounted for 20 per cent of FDI flows. Moreover, countries like Mauritius, Singapore, USA and Japan have accounted for 64 per cent of investment inflows in the Indian states pertaining to infrastructure development schemes and other government initiatives, such as Smart Cities, Industrial Corridor, Ease of Doing Business (EoDB) and High-Speed Rail Projects.[13, 14]

India's growth trajectory in terms of economic collaborations, foreign investments and infrastructure development suggests that paradiplomacy in India is an economic compulsion rather than a diplomatic offshoot. The former minister of external affairs, Sushma Swaraj, has stated that "India's economic interest has acquired a new profile in recent years and has increasingly made foreign policy a tool to assist with domestic economic transformation."[15] Swaraj pointed out that this is "Cooperative and Competitive Federalism" that places emphasis on "states in India to be an integral part of foreign policy" to expand India's economic dimensions.[16] A cooperative and competitive federalism is an approach that has led to the emergence of a new context for the foreign policy of India.

Table 5.1: States/UTs Attracting Highest FDI Equity Inflows

No.	State	% Age to total Inflows (in terms of US$)
1	Gujarat	35%
2	Maharashtra	20%
3	Karnataka	15%
4	Delhi	12%
5	Jharkhand	5%
6	Tamil Nadu	4%
7	Haryana	3%
8	Telangana	3%
9	Uttar Pradesh	1%
10	West Bengal	1%

Source: FDI Factsheet—July to September 2020[17]

Cooperative and Competitive Federalism

Since 2016, the concept of 'cooperative' and 'competitive' federalism has been reflected in India's foreign policy making. Cooperative federalism is defined as the increasing interdependence of federal and regional governments without destroying the principle of federalism; whereas, competitive federalism encourages a healthy competition among state governments that can boost the country's growth trajectory. Prime Minister Modi incorporated this concept in practice with the aim to transform the country "from a single-pillar growth nation to a nation that has 30 pillars of growth: these are the 29 states of India and the federal government."[18] Prime Minister Modi, in his interview with *Time* Magazine, stated that:

> "I wanted the federal government and the state governments to work together for the country. I basically wanted to bring about a complete change in the thinking that the federal government is a giver to the state government and the state government is a recipient of the largesse from/ of the federal government."[19]

Generally, the concept of 'cooperative' and 'competitive' federalism acts as a mechanism to strengthen centre-state coordination in matters related to foreign policy and economic cooperation. It is a strategy where "states spur into greater effort through a healthy competition for economic growth and prosperity."[20] Prime Minister Modi, in one of his speeches at the opening ceremony of the Hannover Messe (2015), said that "this is a new partnership between the centre and the states where we see our Indian states and cities as partners in our international engagement."[21] Cooperative and competitive federalism acts as a forward policy focused on trade and investments that represents Indian states and cities as equal stakeholders in executing economic reforms and ease of doing business in India.[22] Besides, considering the vast population and geographical diversity of India, it is a tough task for the Union government to overcome the challenges posed by the social and economic forces of each state. Although the engagement of the states and cities in foreign interactions increased only in recent years, the awareness for the same was raised decades ago. For instance, former Prime Minister Dr. Manmohan Singh, in his speech on the 58th Independence Day in 2004, stated that:

> "For the benefits of development to reach all corners of the country, the centre and states have to work in a spirit of cooperative federalism. It is the responsibility of the central government to help states to realise our common and shared objectives of development. But there is much that state and local governments can do to promote growth, social justice and welfare. They must raise the required resources to the extent feasible. Equally important, attention must also be paid to the quality and effectiveness of government."[23]

The state governments are aware of their political, economic and social settings. They have a better hand in conducting diplomatic missions in areas of investment, trade, commerce, education, cultural exchanges, FDI and business opportunities. Examples include the launch of the India-US Infrastructure Collaboration Platform and the Japanese support for the Chennai Metro Project, the Mumbai-Ahmedabad Bullet Train project, the Chennai-Bangalore Industrial Corridor and for the improvement of road networks in the north-eastern states of the country. The growing interactions between the state governments and foreign governments suggest that a decentralisation of foreign policy is in progress. The finance minister of India, Nirmala Sitharaman, in a speech, pointed out that, "States have a significant role in building and sustaining a manufacturing revolution and in the spirit of cooperative as well as competitive federalism, they will be the drivers of development and the centre will play a catalytic role."[24] It seems that the state governments will play a proactive role in areas concerning their regional interest in the years ahead.

Due to the increasing paradiplomatic activities by the Indian states and cities within the framework of cooperative and competitive federalism during the last few decades, it became a prerequisite for the government to recognise the involvement of the states in the formulation and implementation of certain aspects of foreign policy. According to Happymon Jacob, "The role of states in India has traditionally been seen by New Delhi as hampering its constitutionally mandated, autonomous, unconstrained foreign policy making process. Today, there is an increasing acceptance of states' legitimate concerns and role."[25] The obvious question is why and how is the involvement of states in foreign/diplomatic affairs a sustainable approach for India? By examining the various initiatives proposed by the Union government to make paradiplomacy viable in India's foreign policy conduct, one can observe a positive trend. The section that follows lists the various institutional arrangements initiated and their role in this direction.

Creation of States Division

In the past few decades, India has become an international diplomatic hub that has proficiently hosted over 100 heads of state/government, vice-premiers, vice-presidents, honorary consul generals, ambassadors/foreign embassies, high-profile diplomatic and business delegations and other well-known international organisations.[26] The constituent states of India have gained importance in hosting international conferences and have played benefactor roles in intensifying the country's paradiplomatic engagements. Apart from Delhi, the foreign officials often wish to visit the Taj Mahal at Agra and other metropolitan cities, such as Mumbai, Hyderabad, Bangalore etc. One can recall that Prime Minister Shinzo Abe of Japan began his visit from Gujarat (Ahmedabad) in 2017, by inaugurating the "508 km long Mumbai-Ahmedabad first high-speed rail project."[27] In October 2009, the Russia-India-

China trilateral meeting was hosted at India's IT city, Bangalore.[28] In 2012, Gurgaon (Haryana) facilitated 20 foreign ministers from the Indian Ocean Rim Association of Regional Cooperation (IOR-ARC). Later, in November 2013, the Asia-Europe Meeting (ASEM) was successful in bringing nearly 50 foreign ministers and senior officers to Gurgaon (Haryana).[29]

In order to efficiently deal with such frequent visits, the MEA established a 'States Division' headed by a Joint Secretary, to coordinate the process between the centre and states. The annual report (2015-2016) of the MEA suggested that the "States have a critical role to play, particularly in the success of commercial and cultural diplomacy."[30] Further, in January 2016, the Inter-State Council Secretariat (ISCS), Ministry of Home Affairs, in collaboration with the Forum of Federations, UNDP, World Bank and CUTS International hosted a conference on cooperative federalism in New Delhi that concentrated on "how to induce states to be more participative and proactive in global affairs."[31] One of the reasons behind creating this Division was to address the issue of the lack of coordination between the centre and states at the implementation level. For example, in 2009, when Japan made a commitment of US$ 100 billion in the Chennai-Bangalore Industrial Corridor and Delhi-Mumbai Industrial Corridor projects, the Japan Chamber of Commerce appealed to the government for an urgent intervention to resolve the differences between the centre and the states.[32]

The States Division is mandated to help the state governments in identifying countries and regions for promoting tourism, cultural and academic exchanges, trade and diaspora outreach. This would further enable the states to shape suitable strategies for maximising the gains from foreign interactions. For instance, the States Division drafted a strategy to assist the states and Union Territories (UTs) to smoothly carry out diplomatic and trade missions in India. In order to bridge the gap between states/UTs and Mission/Posts abroad, the division requested the states/UTs and Heads of Missions to appoint nodal officers to coordinate with each other.[33]

Moreover, due to the desire of more foreign dignitaries to visit cities besides Delhi, the States Division facilitates visits in tier-2 cities. According to Shri Sayed Akbaruddin (official spokesperson), the idea behind this initiative is to consult the Ministry of Home Affairs (MHA) in the decision-making process and provide an explanation of the functioning of the MEA and mechanisms available for them to utilise in promoting economic cooperation. The MEA has asserted that the chief function of this new division is "to facilitate states to expand their external linkages through training and capacity building in areas related to exports, tourism and culture and further attract more overseas investment and expertise."[34] Moreover, as per the decision taken by the MEA, the Officer Trainees (OTs) at the Foreign Service Institute (FSI), New Delhi, have been assigned states to seek further specialisation. This initiative has helped the OTs in understanding the requirement of a particular state through the exchange of dialogues with the respective officers.[35]

The MEA has also set forth guidelines for appointing state protocol officers to handle the visits of foreign dignitaries, consuls, vice-presidents and heads of government at the state level. According to Shri Akbaruddin, various decisions taken by the MEA have a direct impact on the states, such as trade and investments, affairs concerning the state delegations' visit to various countries and political clearances.[36] The visits made by the foreign delegates to the states and UTs are assured by state protocol authorities to maintain a uniform policy. These visits are classified as (a) State visits (b) Official visits and (c) Working visits.

Further, as per the guidelines of the All India Services, the Protocol Officer (P4 level) assists the senior Protocol Officer in providing foreign services that conform to the national policies and practices and international norms and conventions. Besides, the protocol officers also facilitate the foreign officials in important ceremonies and functions at the implementation level.[37] The States Division has facilitated various programmes and foreign visits to encourage the role of the states in India's foreign policy, some of which are listed below:

Table 5.2: Foreign Interactions of Indian State Governments

Date/Year	Interaction of State Governments with Foreign Countries	Purpose/Programme
July 2015	Deputy CM of Punjab's visit to Poland and Hungary	To attract foreign investment in the area of agriculture and processed food
	CM of West Bengal's visit to the UK	To promote investment partnerships and to sign an MoU for urban development and education

	Governor of Aichi Prefecture, Japan's visit to Gujarat and Rajasthan	Investment Summit
August 2015	CM of Haryana's visit to the US and Canada	To promote trade and investment
	CM of Karnataka's visit to Peru and Mexico	Invest Karnataka 2015
September 2015	CM of Maharashtra's visit to Japan	Maharashtra State Investment Promotion Seminar
	CM of Telangana's visit to China	Switzerland-based World Economic Forum (WEF) summit in Dalian
October 2015	CM of Punjab's visit to Poland	Progressive Punjab Investment Summit at Mohali, Punjab
February 2016	Foreign dignitaries' visit to Mumbai	Make in India Summit
March 2016	Nordic Ambassador's visit to Assam, Manipur and Sikkim	To promote cultural interest
October 2016	Foreign dignitaries' visit to Madhya Pradesh	Global Investors Summit at Ujjain
August 2018	CM of Assam's visit to Guangzhou	To promote Assam as an investment destination
September 2018	CM of Andhra Pradesh's visit to New York	To engage with potential investors and companies
August 2019	Foreign dignitaries' visit to Vijayawada, Andhra Pradesh	Diplomatic Outreach Event
September 2019	CMs of Uttar Pradesh, Haryana, Gujarat and Goa's visit to Russia	Eastern Economic Forum
November 2019	Foreign dignitaries' visit to Himachal Pradesh	Rising Himachal Global Investors' Meet
October 2020	Chaired by Secretary (East) on virtual platform	India-Vietnam Business Forum
October 2020	Chief Secretary of Haryana on virtual platform	Forum of Shanghai Cooperation Organization
October 2021	Foreign dignitaries' visit to Chandigarh	Haryana-Africa Conclave: Series-I
November 2022	Foreign dignitaries' visit to Bhubaneshwar	Make in Odisha Conclave
February 2023	Virtual Conference	UP Invest

Source: Ministry of External Affairs (Annual Report 2015-2022).

The above table indicates that the states are playing a unique role in shaping India's global paradiplomacy. Most of these programmes and foreign visits (Table 5.2) are headed by Chief Ministers and other heads of departments of ministries at the state level.[38, 39, 40, 41, 42, 43, 44]

For instance, 'Meet the States' initiative was organised by K.T. Rama Rao, Minister of State for Information Technology of Telangana, to attract foreign investments in Telangana.[45] The delegation in Andhra Pradesh was headed by Ganta Srinivasa Rao, Minister of Human Resource Development and was focused on educational opportunities. The conference was attended by diplomats from Australia, China, Finland, France, Germany, Singapore, Sweden, USA and the UK. Moreover, states have also shown interest in agendas such as climate change.[46] The delegation from Kansai Economic Federation (Kankeiren), Japan, was focused on the "construction of smart cities with low carbon societies and cooperation in areas, such as municipal solid waste management, renewable energy, disaster management, tourism, education and sustainable development."[47] The meeting was chaired by Joint Secretary (States). In order to foster trade and investment, the States Division facilitated the 4th Sudanese International Oil Seeds Conference on 18 November, 2018, in Khartoum, Sudan, which was attended by major companies from Gujarat, Karnataka and Maharashtra.[48]

In the north-eastern region of India, the States Division represented the MEA at the 'North East Connectivity Summit' at Agartala in September 2016, organised by the Federation of Indian Chambers of Commerce and Industry (FICCI), Ministry of Development of North-Eastern Region and Government of Tripura, to promote trade and investment in the North-East through enhanced connectivity.[49] In 2017, delegates from Australia, the Czech Republic, Japan, Malaysia, Mexico, the Netherlands, South Korea, Singapore, Sri Lanka, the Slovak Republic, Syria, Thailand, Vietnam, the UK and the US visited various states and UTs.[50] Furthermore, in 2018, the States Division coordinated with the Ministry of Finance in concluding a proposal of the Government of Assam with the World Bank's support for the implementation of the Assam State Roads Project Phase-II.[51] In the same year, the States Division coordinated the signing of an MoU between the University of California, Berkeley and the state of Arunachal Pradesh and another between the Department of Animal Husbandry & Veterinary, Government of Meghalaya and the Promotion of Animal Production of Wallonia - ProAniWal, Wallonia region, Kingdom of Belgium.[52] In November 2020, the Division had facilitated the meeting of the Ambassador of Israel, Ron Malka, with the Secretary NEC (North-Eastern Council).[53]

In 2018, the States Division had conducted the visits of Presidents, Vice Presidents, Prime Ministers, Ministers, Governors, Mayors and other foreign dignitaries from "Afghanistan, Australia, Indonesia, Malaysia, Nepal, Singapore, Belgium, Bhutan, Canada, the European Union, Sri Lanka, Sweden, Thailand, Nordic Countries and the UAE to various states and union territories in India."[54] In 2019, the Division coordinated the participation of the chief ministers of five Indian states in the Eastern Economic Forum in Vladivostok, Russia.[55] Around 140 Indian companies attended the forum, which focused on strengthening cooperation in the areas of "trade, economy and investment, scientific and technical cooperation."[56] The MoUs were signed between Sakhalin Oblast and Haryana, the Republic of Sakha (Yakutia) and Gujarat, the Republic of Buryatia and Maharashtra, Zabaikalsky Krai and Uttar Pradesh and between Kamchatka Kray and Goa.[57] Furthermore, the Rising Himachal Global Investors' Meet 2019 observed the participation of around 1700 business delegates including 200 international delegates from the UAE, the Netherlands, PIOCCI (People of Indian Origin Chamber of Commerce and Industry), Russia, Vietnam, Germany etc. along with ambassadors from 10 countries.[58] In 2021, the States Division facilitated the Haryana-Africa Conclave Series I to strengthen cooperation between 12 African countries—Ethiopia, Ghana, Malawi, Mozambique, Uganda, Tanzania, Madagascar, Kenya, Nigeria, Eritrea, Zimbabwe and Senegal.[59]

In 2020, the States Division, under its 'Market Expansion Activities' budget, has increased its funding up to 10 crores that allows Indian Missions/Posts to expand its economic activity with countries of their accreditation. The funding was utilised to help promote "Indian exports through catalogue shows and buyer-seller meets, engage consultants to prepare market studies, organise business seminars to attract foreign investments and undertake advocacy work to promote interests of Indian enterprises seeking business opportunities overseas."[60] In 2022, the 2nd North-East Buyer-Seller Meet (BSM) was inaugurated in Guwahati by Himanta Biswa Sarma, the chief minister of Assam, where products from the north-eastern region were exhibited.[61] In the same year, the States Division facilitated the Make in Odisha Conclave that mobilised foreign investment up to 10.5 trillion rupees.[62] Later, in February 2023, the Uttar Pradesh Global Investors Summit was organised that invited policy makers, corporate leaders, business delegations, academicians, think-tanks and political and government leadership from across the globe to bring in foreign investments and develop business partnerships.[63] The state governments, through the creation of the States Division, gained a strong foothold in practicing paradiplomacy at a higher level/on a larger scale. The foreign engagements facilitated by the States Division increased the efficiency within the MEA that eventually helped to smoothen the coordination between the centre and the states.

Sister-City and Sister-State Agreements

Indian states and cities have entered into many sister-city agreements with foreign cities to enhance cooperation and coordination at the local level. The sister- city agreements have further recognised the pivotal role of municipal corporations and local bodies in the decision-making process. In 2017, the MEA finalised the revision of the existing Standard Operating Procedures (SOPs) regarding Memorandum of Understandings (MoUs) and Agreements with foreign countries.[64] Along with 12 new provisions regarding treaty-making formalities, the SOPs also provided guidelines for concluding twinning agreements under two criteria:

a. Guidelines/SOPs concerning the Conclusion of Twinning Agreements with the Provincial Governments of Foreign Countries.
b. Guidelines/SOPs concerning the Twinning Arrangements between the Cities.[65]

The MEA has emphasised the role of state governments and agencies for promoting cooperation in investments, industry, commerce, culture, health, tourism and other areas.[66] The SOPs also assert that "such proposals should be considered on a case-by-case basis by the concerned Administrative Ministry, taking into account the nature, scope and overall usefulness of the understanding being entered into."[67] Moreover, the twinning agreements are to be reviewed annually.

Furthermore, the guidelines have acknowledged the Ministry of Urban Development (MoUD) as the nodal ministry at the central level for concluding Twinning Arrangements between the Indian states and cities and foreign countries. In 2014, the MoUD provided guidelines for 'Twinning of Cities' in an effort "to exchange the expertise and cooperation in the fields of service delivery, civic administration, land use planning and management, transport, shelter, education, culture, sports, waste water and solid waste management, infrastructure, environment, public health, science and technology, tourism, heritage management, urban renewal, urban and regional planning and related matters and other pertinent activities related to sustainable development."[68]

Along with the formal consent of the local government of the foreign city, the twinning arrangements also require the collective involvement of multilateral agencies, government agencies and community-based non-government organisations of the respective country.[69] These agencies could play a dynamic role in fostering city-to-city cooperation as a feasible development model. Furthermore, the local governments and community-based non-government organisations and corporations would facilitate the development of public-private partnerships.[70]

Furthermore, the twinning proposals shall be processed only in Statutory Towns.[71] The MoUD has categorised the maximum number of foreign cities/provinces/states with which the Indian cities may be twinned, based on their population, as follows:

Table 5.3: Categorisation of Indian Cities

Sr. No.	Categorisation of Indian Cities (Population as per census 2011)	Existing Twinning Agreements	Proposed Twinning Agreements
1.	>10 million	4	15
2.	5-10 million	4	10
3.	1-5 million	-	5
4.	0.1-1 million	2	3
5.	Rest of the cities	1	2

Source: Ministry of Urban Development, 2014.

The MEA has also stated that there has been a notable increase in twinning agreements between Indian cities and foreign provinces/cities that has fostered cooperation in "urban development, cultural propagation, heritage conservation and people-to-people links."[72] The Kyoto-Varanasi Partner City Agreement in 2015 between India and Japan was a significant step towards India's role in paradiplomacy.[73] The agreement aimed to "promote cooperation in the fields of sewage management, waste management, water management and urban transportation by drawing upon Japanese expertise and technology."[74] The agreement shall also help Varanasi develop into a smart heritage city. This is also known as smart-city diplomacy.[75]

Table 5.4: List of Sister-City Agreements in India

City/State	Sister-City (year)
Ahmedabad	Astrakhan, Russia (2000); Columbus, USA (2008); Guangzhou, China (2014); Valladoid, Spain (2017); Kobe, Japan (2017); Port Louis, Mauritius; Jersey City, USA
Amravati	Abu Dhabi, Dubai (2017)
Amritsar	Sandwell, UK; Waitakere (2009)
Andhra Pradesh	Sichuan, China (2016); Canton of Zurich (2018)
Aurangabad	Dunhuang, China (2015)
Ayodhya (Faizabad)	Kimhae, South Korea (2000); Janakpur, Nepal (2014)
Almora	Saas Fee, Valais Switzerland (2020)
Assam	Chiang Mai, Thailand (2020)
Bangalore	Minsk, Belarus (1973); Cleveland, USA (1992); San Francisco, USA (2009); Chengdu, China (2013); Nanjing, China
Bikaner	Udine, Italy
Bhavnagar	Loughborough, UK (2016)
Bhubaneshwar	Cupertino, USA (2012)
Bodhgaya	Lumbini, Nepal
Chennai	Volgograd, Russia (1966); Denver, USA (1984); Frankfurt, Germany; San Antonio, USA (2008); Chongqing, China (2015); Kuala Lumpur, Malaysia; Ulsan, South Korea (2016) , Fujian, Guangzhou, China (2020)
Cochin	Norfolk, USA (2010); Menlo Park (2015); Pyatigorsk, Russia
Coimbatore	Toledo, USA (2009); Esslingen am Neckar, Germany (2016)
Chandigarh	Nottingham (2019)
Daman & Diu	Lources, Portugal

Delhi	Chicago, USA (2001); London, UK (2002); Ulaanbaatar, Mongolia (2002); Moscow and St. Petersburg, Russia (2002); Beijing, China (2013); Ottawa, Canada (2016); Leuven, Belgium (2017); Fukuoka, Japan (2018); Seoul, South Korea (2018)
Gujarat	Guangdong, China (2014); California (2001); Hyogo, Japan (2016); New Jersey (2019)
Hyderabad	Riverside, USA (2000); Suwon, South Korea (2005); Miyoshi, Japan (2006); Brisbane and Ipswich, Australia (2010); Indianapolis, USA (2010); Schaumburg, USA (2011); Qingdao, China (2015); Kazan, Russia
Jaipur	Pocheon, South Korea; Calgary, Canada; Adelaide, Australia (2017)
Jalandhar	Union City, USA; London Borough, UK
Jamshedpur	Gunsan City, South Korea (2004)
Jharkhand	Shanxi, China (2016)
Karnataka	Sichuan, China (2013); Bavaria, Germany (2007); Mie (2018)
Khanty-Mansiysk	Okrug-Ugra, Russia (2017)
Kolkata	Kunming, China (2013); Greece
Kozhikode	Sines, Portugal (2020)
Madhubani	Tver, Russia
Maharashtra	Sverdlovsk, Russia (2016)
Mangalore	Hamilton, Canada (1968)
Manipal	Loma Linda, USA (1982); Delta, British Columbia (2010)
Meghalaya	Wallonia, Belgium (2017)
Mumbai	St. Petersburg, Russia (1967); Stuttgart, Germany (1968); Honolulu, Hawaii (1970); Los Angeles, USA (1972); Busan, South Korea (2009); Shanghai, China (2014); Izmir, Turkey; Ho Chi Minh City, Vietnam (2020)
Mysore	Cincinnati, USA (2012)
Nagpur	Jinan, China (2016)
Panjim	Victoria, Seychelles (2018)
Pimpri-Chinchwad	Gunsan City, South Korea (2004)
Port Blair	Phuket, Thailand; Sabang, Indonesia (2020)
Pune	Bremen, Germany (1976); San Jose, USA (1989); Fairbanks, USA (2004); Tromsø, Norway; Toyota, Japan; Vacoas-Phoenix, Mauritius
Sambalpur	Tver, Russia
Shimla	Carbondale, USA (2005)

Telangana	New Jersey (2019)
Thiruvananthapuram	Galveston, USA
Varanasi	Kyoto, Japan (2015); Kathmandu, Nepal (2014)
Vijayawada	Modesto, USA (1993)
West Bengal	Jeollanam-do-Province (2019) and Gyeongnam-do-Province (2019), South Korea

A Memorandum of Cooperation was signed between METI (Ministry of Economy, Trade and Industry of Japan) and the state of Gujarat on 'Japan-India special programme for Make in India' in Mandal Becharaji-Khoraj in Gujarat to facilitate infrastructure development schemes.[76] Currently, India has approximately 100 twinning agreements with foreign states and cities (Table 5.4). India and the US have 23 sister-city agreements (Table 5.4) along with two sister-state agreements with California. In 2015, the Provincial-State Leaders Forum was launched between India and China to encourage subnational cooperation between the two countries. This led to the signing of an agreement on friendship with foreign countries on state/provincial leaders' forum to strengthen exchanges at the municipality level.[77] Another agreement was signed to enhance cooperation between the MEA and the international department of the Central Committee of the Communist Party of China.[78] The forum concluded a sister-state agreement between Karnataka and Sichuan, followed by sister-city agreements between Chennai-Chongqing, Hyderabad-Qingdao and Aurangabad-Dunhuang. Currently, China has 10 sister-city agreements and around four sister-state agreements with India (Gujarat, Andhra Pradesh, Jharkhand and Karnataka). The forum also focused on "cooperation in the development of smart cities with the identification of GIFT City in India and Shenzhen in China as pilot smart cities for joint demonstration projects."[79] In 2016, three municipal corporations of Delhi signed MoUs with Ottawa, Canada, to promote tourism and collaborate on the exchange of technical skills. Furthermore, in 2017, Jaipur signed a MoU with Adelaide (Australia) in the field of smart city initiatives.[80] In 2019, West Bengal signed an agreement on cooperation and the development of friendly relations between Jeollanam-do-Province and Gyeongnam-do Province in South Korea.[81] In 2021, sister-city agreements were concluded between Kozhikode (Kerala) and Sines (Portugal); Almora (Uttarakhand) and Saas Fee (Valais Switzerland); and Mumbai and Ho Chi Minh City (Vietnam).[82]

In the same year, a sister port agreement was concluded between Port Blair and Port of Sabang (Indonesia).[83]

Such agreements have helped the states and cities to develop foreign interactions, but most of these agreements are still under process as some of them still require approval from the state governments.[84] Besides, most of these agreements are based on economic and cultural cooperation, with less focus on strategic issues. Most of these agreements are mainly confined to economic cooperation focused on trade, investments and infrastructure development.

This brings us to conclude that the practice of paradiplomacy in India is mainly an economic compulsion rather than a diplomatic offshoot. The central government's emphasis to increase the states' and cities' engagement in foreign policy in the post-reform period clearly indicates that paradiplomacy became a prerequisite for India to boost its economic strength. Indeed, the creation of the States Division within the MEA facilitated the foreign engagements of states through sister-cities and twinning agreements and MoUs based on trade and economic cooperation. Such agreements have ultimately enhanced the states' and cities' participation in international affairs, making paradiplomacy a necessary practice to expand India's economic realm. Such measures undertaken by the central government within just a decade clearly suggests that India shall continue to aggressively practice paradiplomacy as part of its foreign policy to enhance its global stature in the realm of international diplomacy.

However, the initiatives undertaken by the Indian states and cities are still at a preliminary stage. India is on a steep learning curve to fully incorporate paradiplomacy as part of its foreign policy. Lessons from other countries that have extensively used paradiplomacy as a foreign policy tool can help India make paradiplomacy a dynamic policy in conducting foreign affairs. The next chapter discusses the necessary takeaway for India from countries like China and Brazil, who have made paradiplomacy a catalytic tool in their foreign policy.

Notes

1. Hazarika, "Evolving Dynamics of Federalism and Foreign Policy."
2. Girish Sant and Shantanu Dixit, "The Enron Controversy: Techno-Economic Analysis and Policy Implications," (Prayas: www.prayaspune.org, 1995).
3. Hazarika, "Evolving Dynamics of Federalism and Foreign Policy," p. 6.

4. Prakash Chandra Jha, "Federalism, Regionalism and States' Paradiplomacy in India," in *Federalism in India: Towards a Fresh Balance of Power* ed. Lancy Lobo and Jayesh Shah (Delhi: Rawat Publication, 2014).
5. Hazarika, "Evolving Dynamics of Federalism and Foreign Policy," p. 8.
6. Ibid.
7. Vibrant Gujarat is a biennial investors' summit held by the Government of Gujarat to bring together business leaders, investors, corporations, thought leaders, policy and opinion makers with an aim to explore business opportunities in Gujarat.
8. Hazarika, "Evolving Dynamics of Federalism and Foreign Policy."
9. Ibid.
10. Ratna, T. (November 10, 2013). *Paradiplomacy: A New Way for Indian Foreign Policy?* Retrieved from The Diplomat: https://thediplomat.com/2013/11/paradiplomacy-a-new-way-for-indian-foreign-policy/
11. Prime Minister's Office, "Text of Prime Minister's Inaugural Address at Delhi Economics Conclave," Press Information Bureau, Government of India, November 6, 2015, accessed on June 25, 2016, http://pib.nic.in/newsite/PrintRelease.aspx?relid=130283.
12. DIPP, "Fact Sheet on Foreign Direct Investment (Fdi) from April, 2000 to June, 2017," http://dipp.nic.in/sites/default/files/FDI_FactSheet_June2017_2_0.pdf: Department of Industrial Policy and Promotion, 2017.
13. Ibid.
14. "Fact Sheet on Foreign Direct Investment (FdI) from April, 2000 to September, 2020," in *Quarterly Fact Sheet* (https://dipp.gov.in/sites/default/files/FDI_Fact_sheet_September_20.pdf: Department for Promotion of Industry and Internal Trade, 2020).
15. MEA, "Speech by Minister of State for External Affairs at the Gateway of India Dialogue (June 14)," news release, 2016, http://mea.gov.in/Speeches-Statements.htm?dtl/26910/Speech_by_Minister_of_State_for_External_Affairs_at_the_Gateway_of_India_Dialogue_June_14_2016.
16. Ibid.
17. DIPP, "Fact Sheet on Foreign Direct Investment (FDI) from April, 2000 to September, 2020."
18. MEA, "Prime Minister's Interview to the Time Magazine," news release, 2015, https://www.mea.gov.in/interviews.htm?dtl/25211/prime+ministers+interview+to+the+time+magazine.
19. Ibid.
20. "German Companies Are Welcome," news release, 2015, https://www.mea.gov.in/articles-in-foreign-media.htm?dtl/25060/german+companies+are+welcome.

21. "Prime Minister's Address at the Opening Ceremony of Hannover Messe," news release, 2015, https://www.mea.gov.in/Speeches-Statements.htm?dtl/25059/prime+ministers+address+at+the+opening+ceremony+of+hannover+messe+april+12+2015.
22. "Speech by Minister of State for External Affairs at the Gateway of India Dialogue (June 14)."
23. "Address to the Nation by Prime Minister Dr. Manmohan Singh from the Ramparts of the Red Fort, New Delhi on the 58th Independence Day," news release, 2004, https://www.mea.gov.in/Speeches-Statements.htm?dtl/3414/address+to+the+nation+by+prime+minister+dr+manmohan+singh+from+the+ramparts+of+the+red+fort+new+delhi+on+the+58th+independence+day.
24. "Make in India Week Curtain Raiser," news release, 2016, https://www.mea.gov.in/press-releases.htm?dtl/26334/make+in+india+week+curtain+raiser.
25. Happymon Jacob, "Putting the Periphery at the Center: Indian States' Role in Foreign Policy," Carnegie India, https://carnegieindia.org/2016/10/10/putting-periphery-at-center-indian-states-role-in-foreign-policy-pub-64724.
26. Manish Chand, "Protocol and Diplomacy: Blending Style with Substance," *In Focus* (2014), http://www.mea.gov.in/in-focus-article.htm?23169/Protocol+and+Diplomacy+Blending+style+with+substance.
27. MEA, "India-Japan Joint Statement During the Visit of Prime Minister to Japan," news release, 2016, https://www.mea.gov.in/bilateral-documents.htm?dtl/27599/IndiaJapan_Joint_Statement_during_the_visit_of_Prime_Minister_to_Japan.
28. Chand, "Protocol and Diplomacy: Blending Style with Substance".
29. Ibid.
30. MEA, "Annual Report (2015-2016)," ed. Ministry of External Affairs, https://www.mea.gov.in/Uploads/PublicationDocs/26525_26525_External_Affairs_English_AR_2015-16_Final_compressed.pdf: http://www.mea.gov.in/, 2016.
31. MHA, "International Conference on Cooperative Federalism: National Perspectives and International Experience," Ministry of Home Affairs, Government of India, http://interstatecouncil.nic.in/international-conference-on-cooperative-federalism-national-perspectives-and-international-experience/.
32. Suhasini Haidar, "Mea to Oversee Foreign Investments in States," *The Hindu* 2014.
33. Loksabha, "Question No. 2970, New Division for Centre-State Relations," ed. Ministry of State, http://www.mea.gov.in/lok-sabha.htm?dtl/26812/QUESTION_NO2970_NEW_DIVISION_FOR_CENTRESTATE_RELATIONS: Government of India, 2016.
34. FSI, "State Specialization by Ifs Ots of 2014 Batch."
35. Ibid.

36. Akbaruddin Syed, "Transcript of Media Briefing by Official Spokesperson (March 7)," http://www.mea.gov.in/media-briefings.htm?dtl/23044/transcript+of+media+briefing+by+official+spokesperson+march+07+2014: Government of India, 2014.
37. AIS, "State Protocol Officers Guidelines," (All India Services: Government of India).
38. MEA, "Annual Report (2015-2016)."
39. "Annual Report (2016-2017)," ed. Ministry of External Affairs, http://www.mea.gov.in/Uploads/PublicationDocs/29521_MEA_ANNUAL_REPORT_2016_17_new.pdf: http://www.mea.gov.in/, 2017.
40. "Annual Report (2017-2018)," ed. Ministry of External Affairs, http://www.mea.gov.in/Uploads/PublicationDocs/29788_MEA-AR-2017-18-03-02-2018.pdf: http://www.mea.gov.in/, 2018.
41. "Annual Report (2018-2019)," ed. Ministry of External Affairs, http://www.mea.gov.in/Uploads/PublicationDocs/31719_MEA_AR18_19.pdf: www.mea.gov.in, 2019.
42. "Annual Report (2019-2020)," ed. Ministry of External Affairs, http://www.mea.gov.in/Uploads/PublicationDocs/32489_AR_Spread_2020_new.pdf: www.mea.gov.in, 2019.
43. "Annual Report (2020-2021)," ed. Ministry of External Affairs, http://www.mea.gov.in/Uploads/PublicationDocs/33569_MEA_annual_Report.pdf: http://www.mea.gov.in/, 2021.
44. "Annual Report (2021-2022)," ed. Ministry of External Affairs, http://www.mea.gov.in/Uploads/PublicationDocs/34894_MEA_Annual_Report_2021-22.pdf: http://www.mea.gov.in/, 2022.
45. "Annual Report (2015-2016)."
46. Ibid., p. 183.
47. Ibid.
48. "Annual Report (2018-2019)."
49. "Annual Report (2016-2017)," p. 194.
50. "Annual Report (2017-2018)," p. 200.
51. "Annual Report (2018-2019)."
52. Ibid.
53. "Annual Report (2020-2021)."
54. "Annual Report (2018-2019)."
55. "List of Commercial Documents Signed by Various Russian and Indian Entities on the Sidelines of the Prime Minister's Visit to Vladivostok," news release, 2019, https://www.mea.gov.in/bilateral-documents.htm?dtl/31801/List_of_Commercial_Documents_signed_by_various_Russian_and_Indian_entities_on_the_sidelines_of_the_Prime_Ministers_visit_to_Vladivostok.
56. Ibid.

57. "Annual Report (2019-2020)."
58. Ibid.
59. "Annual Report (2021-2022)."
60. "Annual Report (2019-2020)."
61. "Annual Report (2022-2023)," ed. Ministry of External Affairs, https://mea.gov.in/Uploads/PublicationDocs/36286_MEA_Annual_Report_2022_English_web.pdf:, http://www.mea.gov.in/, 2022.
62. Ibid.
63. Ibid.
64. Sanjay Kumar Verma, "Revision of Sops with Respect to Mous/Agreements with Foreign Countries," http://www.mea.gov.in/images/SOP-forwarding-letter-to-Ministries-with-revised-SOPs.pdf: Government of India, 2017.
65. Ibid.
66. MEA, "Annual Report (2015-2016)."
67. Verma, "Revision of Sops with Respect to Mous/Agreements with Foreign Countries."
68. MoUD, "Guidelines for Twinning of Cities," ed. Ministry of Urban Development, http://moud.gov.in/upload/uploadfiles/files/Final%20revised%20twinning%20guidelines04.pdf: Government of India, 2014, p. 1.
69. Ibid.
70. Ibid.
71. The 2011 Census of India defines towns of two types: statutory town and census town. Statutory town is defined as all places with a municipality, corporation, cantonment board or notified town area committee.
72. MEA, "Annual Report (2015-2016)."
73. Ibid.
74. Ibid.
75. Ibid.
76. METI, "Memorandum of Cooperation between the Ministry of Economy, Trade and Industry (METI) of Japan and the State Government of Gujarat of India on "Japan and India Special Program for Make in India" in Mandal-Becharaji-Khoraj, Gujarat", ed. Trade and Industry Ministry of Economy, http://www.meti.go.jp/press/2017/09/20170915006/20170915006-3.pdf: Japan, 2017.
77. MEA, "Memorandum of Understanding between the Ministry of External Affairs, Republic of India and Chinese People's Association for Friendship with Foreign Countries on Establishment of States/Provincial Leaders' Forum," http://www.mea.gov.in/Portal/LegalTreatiesDoc/CH15B2275.pdf2015.
78. "Memorandum of Understanding on Cooperation between the Ministry of External Affairs of the Republic of India and the International Department

of the Central Committee of the Communist Party of China," http://www.mea.gov.in/Portal/LegalTreatiesDoc/CH15B2083.pdf: Government of India, 2015.

79. "Memorandum of Understanding between the Ministry of External Affairs, Republic of India and Chinese People's Association for Friendship with Foreign Countries on Establishment of States/Provincial Leaders' Forum."
80. "Annual Report (2017-2018)."
81. "Annual Report (2019-2020)."
82. "Annual Report (2020-2021)."
83. "Annual Report (2021-2022)."
84. "Annual Report (2017-2018)," p. 199.

6

A Way Forward: Lessons for India

China's Urban Diplomacy

Given its regional proximity to and territorial conflicts with other countries of the region, China's urban diplomacy is focused on conducting paradiplomatic activities to enhance its cross-border cooperation in Asia. This chapter discusses the key objectives of China's urban diplomacy that lay out an important lesson for India to strengthen its economic development and regional integration in Asia.

At the end of the Chinese Communist Revolution in 1949, the People's Republic of China was formed under the leadership of Mao Zedong. He formulated the doctrine of Maoism, a communist ideology that led to the establishment of the Chinese Communist party (CCP). Since then, the CCP[1] remains the sole ruling party in China. In the 1970s, during the post-Mao period, China undertook a thoughtful approach on its interaction with the external world.[2] The economic reforms of Deng Xiaoping in 1976, considered as 'Opening up of China' or 'Reform Era' or 'New China', greatly contributed to China's poverty alleviation efforts and its economic growth. The introduction of new economic reforms in China was a turning point in its overall foreign diplomatic strategy. Before the reform era, the theme of China's diplomacy was to oppose imperialism, colonialism and hegemonism and to support the nationalist revolutions of the oppressed nations for their independence and liberation.[3] Since the 1970s, the government in China implemented a mandatory centrally planned economy system. China is a unitary political system that vests all its national legislative power in the National People's Congress (NPC) and its Standing Committee. Article 3 of the Chinese Constitution stipulates the division of powers between the central and state institutions and states that "The National People's Congress of the People's Republic of China is the highest organ of state power."[4] Article 89 also stipulates that "The State Council decides the division of labour between central and local division in order to unify the leadership of the work of the national administrative organs at various levels throughout the country. Safeguarding national sovereignty and national interests is the basic principle of urban diplomacy in our cities."[5] The State Council and its Standing Committee do not enact laws, but execute them. The decision-making authority in China solely resides in the state's executive organs and in the CCP.[6] Article 66 of the constitution of the People's Republic of China stipulates that "the local people's committees at all levels throughout the country at all administrative agencies are subject to the State Council."[7] The power of local governments[8] was limited to local people's congresses in their respective administrative regions. As per Article 58, the local governments were entitled to "ensure compliance and enforcement of laws, plan local economic construction, cultural construction, public affairs, plan local economic construction, approve local budgets and final accounts, protect public property, maintain public order, protect civil rights and equal rights of ethnic minorities."[9] Wang Yizhou, a Chinese scholar, explains that during this period (1970s), the concept of 'no small matter in foreign affairs' was often attributed to the traditional diplomatic system.[10] He pointed out that "local governments cannot have any direct or indirect influence on the country's decision-making on foreign relations."[11] However, this changed in December 1978, when the Third Plenary Session of the 11th Central Committee of the Communist Party of China shifted the focus of the Party's work towards "socialist modernisation and set a policy of reform and opening up to the outside world."[12]

Since then, national diplomacy has entered a new phase, with "peace and development" as its central theme. China's diplomacy is proposing and brewing a series of new concepts, establishing and operating new mechanisms and actively innovating diplomatic strategies. Zhou Enlai, former Premier of the People's Republic of China, summed up China's 'New Diplomacy' as a combination of official, semi-official and non-governmental diplomacy.[13] He explained that "Our international activities and foreign work has three aspects: the party, the country and the people. This means that China's new official diplomacy and non-governmental diplomacy is dialectically unified."[14]

Since the 21st century, China's cross-border cooperation with countries and cities has restructured its regional economic space. China has extensively developed its regional economic cooperation with neighbouring countries in the fields of environmental construction, environmental protection and sustainable development through sister-cities and friendship agreements. In 1954, the Chinese People's Association for Friendship with Foreign Countries (CPAFFC) was established as a national people's organisation and is engaged in people-to-people diplomacy.[15]

According to Li Xiaolin (President of the Chinese People's Association for Friendship with Foreign Countries), "the 18th and 19th centuries were the era of dynasty diplomacy, the 20th century is the era of national diplomacy, and the 21st century is the era of people's diplomacy."[16] On May 15, 2014, President Xi Jinping, in his speech at the International Friendship Conference and the 60th anniversary of the Chinese People's Association for Friendship with Foreign Countries, stated that, "For the first time, urban diplomacy was proposed together with civil diplomacy and public diplomacy."[17] He emphasised that "we must vigorously carry out international friendship among cities, promote exchanges between Chinese and foreign local governments and promote the realisation of resource sharing, optimisation of complementary potentials and win-win cooperation".[18]

At present, the CPAFFC has set up 46 friendship associations between China and foreign regions and countries. It has developed friendly cooperative relations with more than 500 non-governmental organisations and institutions in 157 countries.[19] As of 2019, around 2570 sister-cities relations were established with 500 provinces and cities of China in 136 countries.[20] This suggests that the cities are playing an increasingly important role in China's opening-up pattern, and urban diplomacy is becoming a new type of diplomacy in China's foreign policy.

According to Li Xinyu, Director of the Center of International Sister City Exchange (CPAFFC), "Urban diplomacy is a manifestation of the characteristics of civil diplomacy compared with official diplomacy."[21] She explained that they maintain a reciprocal relationship with each other, which means that even if official diplomacy is tense, civil diplomacy still has to continue. Therefore, civil diplomacy is an important supplement of official diplomacy, while non-governmental diplomacy is carried out through friendly exchanges between cities.[22] This was evident during the 1970s, when Sino-Japanese relations were politically tense. Later, a Joint Communique of the Government of Japan and the Government of the People's Republic of China was signed in September 1972 to establish diplomatic ties and normalise relations.[23] Amidst this attempt to enhance their diplomatic channels, the Mayor of Kobe City, Japan, Miyazaki Tatsuo, led a Sino-Japanese friendship youth swimming delegation to China to participate in a Sino-Japanese swimming game. When Zhou Enlai received him, Miyazaki Tatsuo proposed that Kobe City would like to build a port city in China. On June 24, 1973, Tianjin city (China) concluded a sister-city agreement with Kobe (Japan).[24] At that time, as per the instructions of Premier Zhou Enlai, the 'sister city', as customarily called by Japan, was renamed 'friend city' in order to reflect the spirit of equal treatment of cities regardless of size.[25] Since then, China has uniformly used the term 'friendship city' in its sister-city exchanges. China's first pair of international sister-cities with Kobe (Japan) marked the beginning of urban diplomacy.

According to Li Xiaolin, cities have played an active role as the 'home field' of the country's foreign policy.[26] From 1973 to 1978, China established six pairs of international sister-cities, all of which are Japanese cities. They are Tianjin City and Kobe City; Shanghai City and Yokohama City; Xi'an City and Nara City; Shanghai City and Osaka City; Xi'an City and Kyoto City; and Nanjing City and Nagoya City.[27] Since then, more than 250 pairs of sister-cities in China and Japan have been established.[28] Through urban diplomacy, Chinese provinces and cities, local governments, social organisations, non-governmental organisations, companies and individuals increased their foreign engagements. The role of Chinese cities became increasingly prominent in national development strategies and cultural exchanges in order to supplement the country's official diplomacy.[29] In 1979, China signed 14 sister-city agreements with cities in Japan, United States, Australia, the Netherlands and Italy.[30] The local effect of globalisation through foreign investments and local internationalisation through sister-city agreements were the two phenomena that contributed to China's 'New Diplomacy' in that period. Later, in 1982, the constitution was revised to expand the scope and functions of local government under "the people's congress of provinces and municipalities."[31] In 1985, the Ministry of Foreign Affairs of China clarified the status of cities in foreign exchanges, saying, "Friendly cities are an important part of our country's people-to-people diplomacy for mutual cooperation."[32]

In 1992, the CPAFFC established the China International Sister-Cities Federation to coordinate and manage multilateral city exchange channels through the various stages of operationalisation.[33] In 1999, the CPAFFC became a member of the IULA (International Union of Local Authorities)[34] and the UCLG (United Cities and Local Governments). Later, in 2004, Shanghai, Tianjin, Guangzhou State, Hunan and other Chinese provinces, cities and local governments joined the UCLG as founding members.[35] As of 2009, around 12 cities and one province in China have become UCLG members. They include the "cities of Beijing, Shanghai, Tianjin and Chongqing, all of which are municipalities directly under the central government. Other members are Guangdong's provincial capital of Guangzhou and Hainan's provincial capital of Haikou in south China; Zhejiang's provincial capital of Hangzhou in east China; Liaoning's provincial capital of Shenyang and its coastal city of Dalian; Heilongjiang's provincial capital of Harbin and Jilin's provincial capital of Changchun in northeast China; as well as Hubei's provincial capital of Wuhan and the province of Hunan in central China."[36] It is apparent that urban diplomacy has become a driving force in China's new national diplomacy.

Figure 6.1: China's Sister-City Relations with the World (2016)

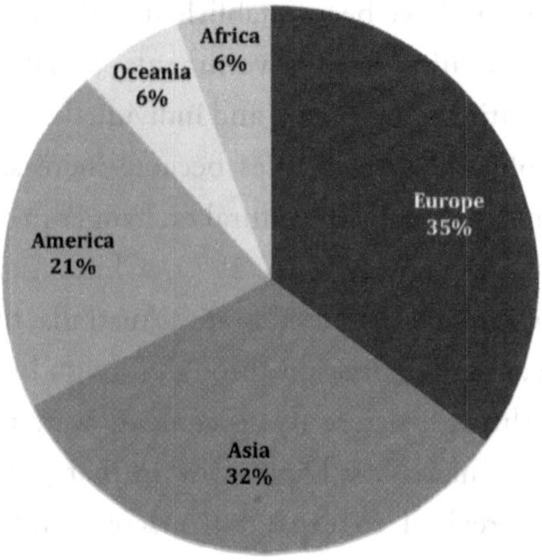

Source: Urban Diplomacy-Theory and Practice (2016).

The report titled "Urban Diplomacy-Theory and Practice" (Li Xiaolin, 2016) highlights the number of China's sister-cities in each continent: there are 776 in Europe, accounting for 35 per cent of the total; 713 in Asia, accounting for 32 per cent of the total; 455 in the Americas, accounting for 21 per cent of the total; 141 in Oceania, accounting for 6 per cent of the total; and 124 in Africa, accounting for 6 per cent of the total. The report concludes that in Africa, sister-cities with China are relatively widespread and 124 cities in two-thirds of the African countries have established international sister-city relations with Chinese cities.[37] In Middle East Asia, the sister-city tie-ups with China are low and only 6 out of 14 countries have established ties with Chinese cities. In Latin America, although the total number of sister-cities with China is relatively high, they are not widely distributed and half of the countries have not established sister-city relations with Chinese cities.[38]

During the past 40 years, China has mainly developed sister-city agreements with developed countries, with an aim to learn urban construction and economic development from the advanced economies of developed countries like Japan, the United States, South Korea, Russia, Australia, France, Germany, Italy and Canada.[39] China has established 1366 pairs of sister-cities among the 35 developed countries in the world (as defined by the International Monetary Fund), accounting for 62.09 per cent of the total number of sister-cities in China.[40] China's focus is to further strengthen its sister-city relations with developing countries in Africa, the Middle East, Latin America, Central and Eastern Europe, Central Asia and other regions to complement each other's advantages, help each other develop and create prosperity together. The report stated that China's urban diplomacy will shift from focusing on "getting" to actively "giving" mutual assistance and a win-win cooperation.[41] China's urban diplomacy is focused on exchange activities between China and foreign sister-cities, which are mainly concentrated in the fields of culture, trade, education and politics. The Blue Book "Special Report on China's Urban Competitiveness (1973-2015)", sponsored by the CPAFFC, outlined/stated that these four fields of exchange activities accounted for 65 per cent of all the exchanges. More than 20 per cent of the exchanges were mainly in the political field.[42] Although the Chinese cities and provinces have played a big role in promoting economic, cultural and social development, it is limited to fulfilling the national interest.

The statutes within the CPAFFC emphasise that the establishment of friendly city relations with foreign countries should go through strict approval procedures.[43] Therefore, from the perspective of the Chinese constitution, the foreign affairs authorities of local governments in China must follow the unified leadership of the central government. Local provinces and cities establish sister-city relations with foreign countries and the relevant provinces, autonomous regions and municipalities directly under the central government. The agreements are approved by the government and are reported to the CPAFFC for scrutiny. They are then transferred to the Ministry of Foreign Affairs for final approval.

To analyse how the international role of the city is subordinate to the country's overall diplomacy, Li Xiaolin has stated three main aspects of urban diplomacy:

1. The role of the city's international economy in promoting the country's hard power
2. The role of the city's international culture in promoting the country's hard power and promotion of soft power
3. The city's international political role in promoting the country's diplomatic power.

On the role of Chinese local governments in the international economy, the Chinese scholar, Chen Zhimin, points out that "In China, attracting foreign direct investment is part of the national development strategy. By granting certain levels of approval power to the local governments, they were mobilised to demonstrate their abilities and attract investment, although there has been some vicious competition with each other. In general, the introduction of foreign capital by the local governments has been very effective, which has contributed greatly to the promotion of China's economic self-reliance."[44] Under the broad policy of 'China's economic construction', many local governments in China, under the guidance of the central government, have actively carried out foreign economic exchanges, attracted investment and promoted cooperation and development.[45] For example, in October 2005, the first Sino-French local government cooperation high-level forum was held in Wuhan. Approximately 200 people from more than 30 regions, provinces and cities across the country attended the meeting. This activity strongly promoted the local governments of China and France. In particular, the positive interaction and cooperation between Wuhan and these local governments expanded Wuhan's international influence. By the end of 2014, the Sino-French local government cooperation high-level forum successively resulted in two pairs of friendship cities between Wuhan and Bordeaux, Nanjing and Strasbourg.[46]

According to Liu Gengyin, the former vice-chairman of the CPAFFC, "the goal of urban diplomacy is not only to safeguard local interests, but also to realise national interests. The balance of interests between national interests and local interests is the body of the relationship between the central and local governments in the field of diplomacy and foreign affairs."[47] The layout of Chinese cities' foreign exchanges has empowered cities like Beijing and Shanghai that are progressing towards the ranks of world cities. Both cities have become nodal centres of the global urban system, with important international influence in the fields of global economy, politics, culture etc. According to the Chinese scholar, Huang Renwei, the significance of building a world city is to serve mutual promotion and mutual cause for the country.[48] A series of urban diplomacy practices in Beijing and Shanghai show that urban diplomacy has greatly promoted the development of the country and the realisation of national diplomatic goals have opened up a broad scope for the internationalised strategy of Chinese cities. For instance, both Beijing and Shanghai are the headquarters of a considerable number of important international organisations and multinational companies. In 2008, Beijing successfully hosted the Olympic Games.[49] In 2010, Shanghai hosted the World Expo 2010 (EXPO Shanghai 2010) to provide foreign countries and companies a chance to develop business partnerships with Chinese companies.[50] Shanghai has also hosted the Shanghai Cooperation Organization Development Bank and is the headquarters of the BRICS Development Bank. The China (Shanghai) Free Trade Zone Pilot (FTZ) was established in 2013 to boost "trade and investment, improve governance and promote financial innovation, leading to impressive achievements in the country's institutional innovation."[51] Since its establishment in Pudong (Shanghai), the Shanghai FTZ has made notable contributions to Pudong's economic transformation and development, with its GDP exceeding 1.27 trillion Yuan in 2019.[52] The Asian Infrastructure Investment Bank (AIIB), initiated and established by China, is located in Beijing and Shanghai, which has helped the cities in providing infrastructure facilities, promote the development of urban economy and tertiary industry and develop a humanistic environment. Huang Renwei believes that the goal of the world city is to continue to advance China's spatial radius in the world market and expand China's cultural cohesion throughout the globe.[53]

The development of urban diplomacy is the driving force to build the international image of Chinese cities through the popularisation of Chinese culture and style.[54] The cultural influence of China has enhanced the country's soft power and demonstrates distinctive Chinese characteristics in foreign affairs. For instance, in June 2007, former Premier Wen Jiabao made a visit to Japan as an 'ice-melting trip' to deepen the historical connection between China and Japan. In his speech, he said, "To advance friendship and cooperation, we need to inherit and carry forward the historical tradition of the long-standing China-Japan friendship. In the course of over 2000 years of interactions, the Chinese nation and the Japanese nation have promoted their respective development and progress by drawing on each other's strengths."[55]

A standing statue of Jianzhen was presented to the Toshodaiji Temple (Japan) to strengthen the relationship between the two countries. Jianzhen was a Chinese monk from Yangzhou city of China, who propagated Buddhism as a religion in Japan.[56] Many Japanese people rushed to witness the style of Jianzhen's standing statue. The stone lantern is exhibited at the Jianzhen Memorial Hall in the Daming Temple of Yangzhou city of China. It was presented in 1980 and lit by Monk Morimoto Takayori from Japan's Toshodaiji Temple, where another stone lantern stands.[57] "With ever-burning lights, this pair of lanterns echo each other from afar and symbolise the bright future of the eternal friendship between the Chinese and Japanese peoples."[58] The then Chinese ambassador to Japan, Wang Yi, commented, "This is successful urban diplomacy, non-governmental foreign affairs diplomacy and cultural diplomacy. Through this, more people can learn about Yangzhou and understand the whole China."[59] This is a typical example of strengthening the country's soft power through urban diplomacy.

Furthermore, in May 2015, during Indian Prime Minister Narendra Modi's visit to China, his first stop was in Xi'an in Shaanxi province. This is because when President Xi Jinping came to India in September 2014, Modi had invited Xi Jinping to visit his hometown in Gujarat where he had started his political career in 2001 as the chief minister of the state.[60] At that time, Xi Jinping sent an invitation to Modi to invite him to Xi'an. Shaanxi has deep significance for Xi Jinping as he "experienced his political awakening when he was sent there in 1969."[61] He later joined the Chinese Communist Party and formed the 'Shaanxi Gang' of confidantes, which later helped him consolidate power. Modi then visited the Big Wild Goose Pagoda temple that has preserved "Buddhist texts and relics brought from India by the Chinese monk, Xuanzang that mentioned his visit to Nalanda (India)."[62] His voyage was "immortalised in 'Journey to the West'—one of the most famous novels in Chinese culture."[63] Xi'an is the best testimony of the historical origins of friendly exchanges between China and India.

In 2014, Xi Jinping, in his speech at the Conference on Work Relating to Foreign Affairs, stated that China should "conduct diplomacy with a salient Chinese feature and a Chinese vision."[64] Xi Jinping has often reiterated that China needs to carry out "major country diplomacy with Chinese characteristics."[65] The term was introduced along with China's 'One Belt One Road' initiative that was launched in 2013. Xi Jinping, during his visit to Central Asia and the South-East Asian countries, proposed the 'One Belt One Road' strategic concept, including the 'Silk Road', 'Economic Belt' and '21st century Maritime Silk Road' and emphasised the need to "carry out urban exchanges and cooperation, and enjoy welcoming the friendship between important cities of countries along the route, focusing on cultural exchanges, and emphasising pragmatism cooperation to form more vivid examples of cooperation."[66] Xi Jinping has stated that,

> "China will continue to open to the outside world in an all-round way, promote mutually beneficial cooperation with countries around the world, promote the construction of the Silk Road Economic Belt and the 21st century Maritime Silk Road, and realise the co-creation and sharing of development opportunities among all countries. China will vigorously carry out cultural exchanges between China and foreign countries and contribute to the advancement of human civilisation."[67]

Since its inception in 2013, the 'One Belt One Road (OBOR)' initiative has enabled Chinese cities to enter all countries in their foreign exchanges. The OBOR, now referred to as the Belt Road Initiative (BRI), runs through the "continents of Asia, Europe and Africa, connecting the vibrant East Asia economic circle at one end and developed European economic circle at the other and encompassing countries with huge potential for economic development. The Silk Road Economic Belt focuses on bringing together China, Central Asia, Russia and Europe (Baltic region); linking China with the Persian Gulf and the Mediterranean Sea through Central Asia and West Asia; and connecting China with Southeast Asia, South Asia and the Indian Ocean."[68] "The 21st century Maritime Silk Road is designed to go from China's coast to Europe through the South China Sea and the Indian Ocean in one route, and from China's coast through the South China Sea to the South Pacific in the other."[69] The report by the National Development and Reform Commission (Ministry of Foreign Affairs, 2015) states, "On land, the Initiative will focus on jointly building a new Eurasian Land Bridge and developing China-Mongolia-Russia, China-Central Asia-West Asia and China-Indochina Peninsula economic corridors by taking advantage of international transport routes, relying on core cities along the Belt and Road and using key economic industrial parks as cooperation platforms."[70] The BRI initiative is an attempt to "carry out exchanges and cooperation among cities, encourage major cities in these countries to become sister-cities, focus on promoting practical cooperation, particularly cultural and people-to-people exchanges and create more lively examples of cooperation."[71]

The report states that the BRI will lead to the opening up of cities, such as Lanzhou and Xining and develop the Ningxia Inland Opening-up Pilot Economic Zone to "establish strategic channels, trade and logistics hubs and key bases for industrial and cultural exchanges opening to Central, South and West Asian countries."[72] The BRI will reach out to Inner Mongolia's proximity to upgrade the railway links connecting Heilongjiang Province with Russia and the regional railway network.[73] This will underpin cooperation between China's Heilongjiang, Jilin and Liaoning provinces and Russia's Far East region on sea-land multi-modal transport.[74] The report states that a "Eurasian high-speed transport corridor linking Beijing and Moscow is being constructed with the goal of building key windows opening to the north."[75]

The BRI would also intensify the construction of ports in coastal cities, such as Shanghai, Tianjin, Ningbo-Zhoushan, Guangzhou, Shenzhen, Zhanjiang, Shantou, Qingdao, Yantai, Dalian, Fuzhou, Xiamen, Quanzhou, Haikou and Sanya.[76]

Cities are the fulcrum of the BRI initiative as the international corridors will mainly rely on central cities that are supported by "policy communication, facility connectivity, unimpeded trade, financing and people-to-people bonds."[77] Cities along the BRI will become the pioneers of China's new strategy of two-way opening up: the central and western regions will "become the frontiers of opening up to the outside world, contributing to economic factors."[78] This two-way opening up would strengthen industries in China and bring development opportunities. China is keen "to implement a more proactive opening strategy, strengthen interactive cooperation between the East, China and the West and comprehensively improve the open economy structure."[79] The BRI mainly involves 18 provinces (autonomous regions/ municipalities directly under the central government) including Xinjiang, Shaanxi, Gansu, Ningxia, Qinghai and Inner Mongolia; six provinces (autonomous regions) in Northwest China; three provinces in Northeast China, which are Heilongjiang, Jilin and Liaoning; Guangxi in Southern China; Yunnan and Tibet in the Southwest; five provinces in the southeast of Shanghai; Fujian; Guangdong; Zhejiang; and Hainan. The BRI also proposes to involve ten inland cities, which are Xi'an, Lanzhou, Xining, Chongqing, Chengdu, Zhengzhou, Wuhan, Changsha, Nanchang and Hefei.[80]

In 2017, the CPAFFC and Fuzhou Municipal People's Government jointly established the 21st century Maritime Cooperation Committee, a standing committee of the United Cities and Local Governments Asia-Pacific (UCLG ASPAC). The Committee will work with the coastal cities and local governments in the Asia-Pacific and the world at large "to build together the 21st century Maritime Cooperation Center, to set up the effective dialogue and linkage mechanism, to serve as an important platform of Belt and Road for the cities and local governments in Asia-Pacific and the world at large to share ideas and best practices on maritime cooperation and to bring forth the development of the core area of the 21st century Maritime Silk Road."[81] The Communiqué of the Fifth Plenary Session of the 18th central Committee of the Communist Party of China in 2015 clearly indicates to improve the strategic layout of opening up, promote two-way opening up and support coastal areas to fully participate in the "global economic cooperation and competition, cultivate advanced manufacturing bases and economic zones with global influence and improve cross-border economic cooperation."[82]

China believes that there will be a demand for regional economic integration and cooperation. The cities in the neighbouring countries of China are at the core of the BRI and Maritime Silk Route initiative in China's new regional strategy of opening up of coastal and border areas and sub-regional cooperation. China is a neighbour to the highest number of countries in the world. There are as many as 29 neighbouring countries (including 14 land-bordering neighbouring countries). In addition, China has 15 coastal provinces (autonomous regions directly under the central government, special administrative regions) and nine coastal provinces.

In the case of East Asia, China's local provinces and cities have played a positive role in Asian regional cooperation. For instance, Southwestern provinces, such as Yunnan and Guangxi, have been the most active regions in participating in sub-regional cooperation.[83] The deepening of international cooperation between Guangxi, Yunnan and the ASEAN countries has led to the Southwestern region's participation in regional integration. As early as 1992, under the initiative of the Asian Development Bank, the six countries of the Greater Mekong Subregion (GMS) held their first ministerial level meeting. Yunnan Province has been the only Chinese participant in China that the GMS cooperates with. The meeting jointly initiated the Great Mekong Sub-region Economic Cooperation (Great Mekong Sub-region) that became instrumental in strengthening the economic ties between countries and boosted economic and social development in the sub-region. In 2006, Nanning (Guangxi) hosted the first Pan-Beibu Gulf Economic Cooperation Forum, with the main focus on cooperation between China and the Association of Southeast Asian Nations (ASEAN).[84] The Seventh Plenary Session of the 10th Committee announced that Nanning will be built "to play an important role in the open cooperation between China and ASEAN as a regional international city with strong regional competitiveness and influence." The ASEAN Mekong Basin Development Cooperation has affirmed Yunnan's role as the main body of China's participation in the development of the ASEAN-Mekong River Basin.[85] The status of Yunnan and Guangxi as sub-national entities in sub-regional cooperation has been recognised by ASEAN. Furthermore, the launch of the China-ASEAN Free Trade Area has pushed Guangxi and Yunnan to open to the outside world.

In the Northwestern province, the establishment of the Shanghai Cooperation Organization and the country's western development strategy has made Xinjiang prominent in promoting regional economic cooperation in Central and Western Asia. There are three main mechanisms for Xinjiang's participation in regional cooperation in Central Asia, namely, the Shanghai Cooperation Organization Economic Cooperation Mechanism, Central Asia Regional Economic Cooperation Mechanism and Sino-Russian Harmony Altai Regional Economic Cooperation Mechanism.[86] Some of these mechanisms are at the national level and some, at the local level. Central Asia's regional economic cooperation was initiated by the Asian Development Bank in 1996 and a formal cooperation was established in 2002. The Altai Regional Economic Cooperation refers to cooperation between the regions surrounding the Altai Mountains, which are China, Russia, Mongolia and Kazakhstan. In April 2003, the International Coordinating Committee for Regional Cooperation between China, Russia, Kazakhstan, Mongolia, Xinjiang and Urumqi was formally established as "four countries and six parties" to promote regional economic prosperity, social progress and sustainable development. Xinjiang is an important participant in this mechanism. The central government has authorised Xinjiang to expand the right to operate land border trade and delegate the power to approve foreign investment projects.[87] The aim of this cooperation is to promote economic cooperation through friendship-cities, communicate with people and culture, eliminate or reduce the security pressure brought on by the forces of terrorism, separatist movements and social instability in the border zone and effectively promote peace and friendship with neighbours.[88]

China's establishment of friendship-cities and sister-cities under the umbrella of China's urban diplomacy has paved the way for its urban development and economic cooperation. Similarly, India's paradiplomatic activities have also achieved some economic cooperation and attracted foreign investments. China's practice of paradiplomacy is quite forceful and influential when compared to India's conduct of the same. Although China and India have different governance structures, there are certain paradiplomatic attempts set out by China, which can help India in making paradiplomacy an effectual foreign policy within Asia and across the globe.

Based on the analysis above, one can find that China has extensively used sister-city exchanges to open up its cities for foreign investments. China has engaged in sister-city agreements mainly with developed countries to strengthen its cities' international influence. Drawing lessons from the Chinese practice of paradiplomacy, India needs to aggressively pursue sister-city agreements with advanced economies to gain investment opportunities and urban development. Through China's urban diplomacy, cities like Beijing and Shanghai have become global cities and international cultural capitals. Following the Chinese model, Indian mega cities like Mumbai, Bangalore and Delhi, through sister-city agreements, can become global cities in the future. The Chinese concept of paradiplomacy has asserted its cultural diplomacy across the world. This study has attempted to uncover certain instances of how China has projected its culture and style through friendship-city exchanges. India, being a culturally diverse country, can spread its influence through paradiplomatic activities. The establishment of sister-city agreements with the Southeast Asian countries through cultural and civilisational linkages can strengthen India's soft power diplomacy. Given India's historical connection with countries like Afghanistan, Iran, Pakistan, Myanmar, Vietnam, Laos and Cambodia, it has great potential to increase its soft power influence through paradiplomacy in South Asia, East Asia and West Asia.

Paradiplomacy can be an effective mechanism to enhance cross-border interaction and regional cooperation within Asia. China has already adopted this concept to effectively use sister-city agreements to promote its BRI initiative. As discussed already, Chinese cities through the BRI and Maritime Silk Route have been the core of sub-regional cooperation and economic activities in Central Asia, Russia and Southeast Asia. In this aspect, India is yet to develop paradiplomatic policies that can perceive its role in regional and economic integration. Like China, around 14 Indian states share borders with seven neighbouring countries, out of which many have cross-border conflicts and social instability. India needs to develop an organisational structure where the state and the centre establish procedures on how to conduct sister-city relations with the neighbouring countries. For instance, China has established organisations like the CPAFFC that has successfully established sister-cities and friendship exchanges within Asia and across the globe. China has also set out regulations on the management of sister-city networks. These regulations contain general provisions, 43 Articles and seven supplement provisions that outline how to conduct international sister-city relations. The regulations provide detailed procedures and templates for local governments to follow while concluding agreements with foreign cities. Although India has established the 'States Division' within the MEA to conduct paradiplomatic activities, there is no specific mandate or provisions prescribed for the state governments to carry out sister-city agreements. The procedure and guidelines provided by the MEA are at a preliminary stage. For instance, in China, once a sister-city agreement is established, the local governments are required to provide an annual report on the performance of the sister-city exchanges to the central government. Each agreement undergoes a review to oversee the objectives and goals achieved within the stipulated period of time. The agreement is renewed only when it meets the requirements proposed by the central government. In the case of India, due to a lack of institutional and standard provisions to regulate the paradiplomatic activities, most of the sister-city agreement performances are not reviewed annually.

This indicates that India needs to institutionalise paradiplomacy with a proper mandate within its foreign policy establishment. The concluding chapter provides suggestions and recommendations on how to make paradiplomacy effective in India.

Paradiplomatic Structures of Brazil

The municipal foreign policy of Brazil lays out important lessons for India in establishing a proper structure to carry out paradiplomatic activities at the local level. The chapter explores how Brazil, through its paradiplomatic structures, has effectively increased its presence in international relations.

Brazil's political structure is that of a federal republic. The country is politically and administratively composed of a Union, states, a Federal District and municipalities, all of which function autonomously under the constitution. The Union comprises "federal territories; their creation, transformation into states or reincorporation into their states of origin is regulated by law."[89] "Each state is governed by its own constitution and is headed by a governor. The country is sub-divided into 26 states and 5,560 municipalities."[90]

In Brazil, the phenomenon of paradiplomacy was recognised in the early 1990s during the "re-democratisation of the Brazilian political and civil society that led to the promulgation of the new 1988 Constitution."[91] The 1964 coup d'état in Brazil "overthrew the reformist government of President João Goulart and had established an authoritarian regime controlled by the armed forces that lasted until 1985."[92] The military installed a "tutelary authoritarian regime to control civil society and the political system, serving as a political model for similar regimes in Latin America during the Cold War."[93] However, this changed in the 1980s as the structural changes brought economic and domestic transformations in the developing nations. Arising from the intense popular outcry after 21 years of military dictatorship, the Federal Constitution adopted in 1988 was the first in the country's history to include amendments by ordinary citizens and representative entities.[94] Due to this, "the decentralisation architecture of the Brazilian federation were approved in the new constitutional system."[95] In contrast to the authoritarianism of the previous period, the new constitution empowered the subnational entities in Brazil's foreign policy.

The structural changes near the end of the Cold War resulted in "increased development of non-state actors; development of new territories, diversified political identities and globalization."[96] The sudden shift in the state-centric political order led to new patterns of economic integration in Brazil. This enabled Brazil to give prominence to the practice of paradiplomacy in its foreign policy conduct. In the 1980s, Brazil developed its first bureaucratic structures within subnational governments to handle international relations. In 1983, the state of Rio de Janeiro, under its governor, Leonel Brizola, established its first consultancy focused on international relations followed by Rio Grande do Sul in 1987.[97] Under the Brazilian constitution of 1988, Article 21 states that "the federal government has the power to maintain relations with foreign states and international organisations."[98] Furthermore, Article 22 lists the exclusive powers of the federal government, but rules out foreign engagements. This paved the way for Brazilian cities and regions to engage in foreign affairs.[99] The constitutional system of Brazil does not legally acknowledge the legitimacy of foreign engagements conducted by subnational governments. "Municipalities and federate-states of Brazil are given a series of complementary and exclusive responsibilities. Nevertheless, there are (is) no constitutional statement that forbids them from developing international activities."[100] The approval of the Constitution has led to an increase in international relations structures within states and municipalities. Most of the subnational governments with a certain type of institutional international relations structure were "concentrated along the South-Southeast axis—the country's economically most developed area."[101]

In 1995, the Ministry of Foreign Affairs took its first steps in accepting foreign engagements by subnational governments as a "normal" dimension of Brazilian foreign policy. During President Fernando Henrique Cardoso's term, Brazilian diplomats came up with the concept of 'federative diplomacy' (equivalent to paradiplomacy), which legitimised the foreign affairs of Brazil's subnational governments focused on business opportunities and cooperation. The diplomats who came forth with this concept clarified that "federative diplomacy means not only the trend towards individual international activity by subnational Brazilian governments, but also encourages their involvement by channeling the demands of non-central governments in the decision-making process of the central government's foreign policy."[102]

The establishment of international offices was imperative for promoting activities abroad by subnational governments. This ultimately created a three-tier federal system, in which the central government, states and municipalities are federated entities.[103] Although foreign affairs remains the exclusive responsibility of the executive, the federated units, with regard to local development, are assigned to seek funds abroad, including the signing of aid agreements with foreign subnational governments.[104] Currently, there are 27 state governments and the governments of about 30 large or medium-sized cities that possess some type of coordinating or advisory structure in the area of international relations. Furthermore, there are 20 other cities that regularly carry out foreign activities of some substance despite lack of specific structures for this purpose.[105] Specific paradiplomatic structures (Table 6.1) were developed only in 2003 after Partido dos Trabalhadores (Workers' Party) came to power at the federal level.[106] The coordinating body for international relations and protocol set up by the party was for arranging the mayor's trips abroad, dealing with protocol issues related to visits by foreign visitors and maintaining contact with foreign officials stationed at the consulates in the city. In 2005, a constitutional amendment known as 'PEC da Paradiplomacia' was proposed, which would allow states and municipalities to conclude agreements or arrangements with their foreign equivalent, with the authorisation of the Union.[107] At present, the proposal is under consideration by the Brazilian National Congress, which states that "federate-states, the Federal District (Brasilia) and municipalities would count on constitutional support in the development of their international strategies and agreements of technical cooperation with their international partners."[108]

Table 6.1: Brazilian Cities with Paradiplomatic Structures

Cities	Structure	Cities	Structure
Camaçari	IR Secretariat Directly under the Governor's Secretariat	Belo Horizonte	IR Service under a Secretariat
Fortaleza	Councillor/Coordinator	Campinas	Municipal IR Secretariat
Recife	IR Service under a Secretariat	Diadema	IR Service under a Secretariat
Salvador	IR Service under a Secretariat	Guarulhos	Councillor/Coordinator
Belem	Councillor/Coordinator	Itú	Municipal IR Secretariat
Boa vista	Councillor/Coordinator	Jundiaí	IR Service under a Secretariat
Rio Branco	Councillor/Coordinator	Osasco	Councillor/Coordinator
Caxias do Sul	IR Service under a Secretariat	Rio de Janeiro	Councillor/Coordinator
Curitiba	IR Service under a Secretariat	Santo André	IR Service under a Secretariat
Florianopolis	Councillor/Coordinator	Santos	Councillor/Coordinator
Foz do Iguaçu	Municipal IR Secretariat	S. Bernardo do Campo	IR Secretariat together with other issues
Joinville	IR Service under a Secretariat	S. José do Rio Preto	IR Service under a Secretariat
Porto Alegre	IR Secretariat together with other issues	São Paulo	Municipal IR Secretariat
Santa Maria	IR Secretariat together with other issues	Sorocaba	IR Service under a Secretariat
		Vitória	Councillor/Coordinator

Source: Cities and Global Governance (2011).

Although paradiplomacy is not fully institutionalised within Brazil's constitutional system, this does not inhibit the performance of subnational entities in foreign affairs. For instance, many federate-states and municipalities have increased their global presence through national associations, such as the National Confederation of Municipalities (Confederação Nacional de Municípios, CNM). The CNM was established in 1980 as the largest municipal entity in Latin America to consolidate the municipal movement and strengthen the autonomy of the municipalities.[109] In 1989, the National Front of Mayors (Frente Nacional de Prefeitos, FNP) was created based on the political articulation of a group of mayors from some capital cities and was institutionalised later in 1999. The purpose of this organisation is to ensure the constitutional principle of municipal autonomy, aiming to guarantee full participation for the municipalities in the federative pact and to conduct foreign activities within the scope of the powers of the executive, legislative and judiciary through collective measures. Furthermore, the FNP also aims to promote the active participation of local entities in urban issues and their engagement in democratic dialogues with the three branches of government at the state and federal levels and with organised civil society.[110] Such organisations have recognised and steered the global presence of Brazilian cities. These organisations conduct "seminars, training courses and publish guides for the development of international projects."[111]

After 1985, the governments of Brazil and Argentina had moved away from geopolitical rivalry for regional collaboration. Both were interested in a platform that would allow their international reintegration. With this in mind, the creation of the Southern Common Market (Mercosur) was attempted in 1991, which later included Paraguay and Uruguay. Mercosur is considered to be the most successful regional integration in the subcontinent. Among the changes that it made possible is the greater interaction between the local governments of its member countries.[112] In 1995, Mercociudades was established to form a regional network of cities by unifying groups of municipalities of countries that are part of Mercosur, with an aim to enhance its regional integration process in South America at the local level through development and cooperation between them. The organisation that started with 12 member cities currently comprises 359 member cities from 10 countries, such as Argentina, Brazil, Paraguay, Uruguay, Venezuela, Chile, Bolivia,

Ecuador, Peru and Colombia.[113] These cities are joined by two states of Brazil (Minas Gerais and São Paulo) and the province of Ecuador (Tungurahua).[114]

Later, in 2005, Brazil launched a forum of international relations municipal secretaries to increase foreign interaction among its subnational entities.[115] Furthermore, South-South international cooperation was one of the prime concerns of Brazilian foreign policy that required all three levels of government to be effective. Hence, the local dimension was given importance in cooperation forums, such as the IBSA (India, Brazil and South Africa). In January 2008, a Local Governance Forum (IBSA 2008) was set up to stimulate cooperation among the subnational governments of the three participating countries.[116]

The subnational governments in Brazil have demonstrated a proactive role in the realm of transnational cooperation. For instance, in 1994, the Special Department for International Cooperation and Fund Raising was founded by the city of Porto Alegre. The city has conducted several international conferences on democratic urban management. In 1996, the United Nations declared Porto Alegre as "one of the forty urban innovations worldwide to be presented at the Second Conference on Human Settlements (Habitat II)."[117] Porto Alegre has become one of the most active subnational foreign policy governments in Brazil. Porto Alegre has succeeded in practicing "public resource distribution known as Participatory Budgeting (Orçamento Participativo), the creation of the Forum of Local Authorities for Social Inclusion (FAL) in 2001 and the creation of the FAL network in 2005."[118] The Municipal International Relations Secretariat of São Paulo, established in 2001 under Mayor Marta Suplicy, is a prototype for all foreign relations offices in Brazil. Marta Suplicy had played a significant role in the international local governments' movement. Belo Horizonte, in 2003, opened its international relations department and gained an informal leadership position at the annual meetings in 2005 of the heads of Brazil's municipal international relations offices where leaders discussed common interests, such as the possibility of giving constitutional authority to the international activities of Brazil's subnational governments.[119]

Later, cities like Salvador, Palmas and Recife also created their own international relations bodies in 2005, which broke the semi-monopoly of the cities of the South/Southeast on paradiplomatic activities.[120] Salvador stands out for having created the largest municipal international relations body in Brazil. Curitiba has also set up an International Relations and Protocol Secretariat in 2005.[121] Curitiba is probably the Brazilian municipality, which is most often visited by international delegations of local governments from all over the world. In 2007, 96 delegations from 23 countries visited Curitiba. The foreign delegates were interested in learning the different aspects of Curitiba's town planning, particularly the public transportation and solid waste recycling systems, for which the city is well-known.[122]

Due to the growing foreign interaction of municipalities and federate-states, the Ministry of External Relations (*Itamaraty*) has established a special administrative service in 2003 at the federal level called *the Assessoria de Relações Federativas* (ARF).[123] The ARF directly comes under the authority of the Minister of Foreign Affairs. This service was later rebuilt as the Council of Federative and Parliamentary Issues (AFEPA). The ARF aims to "create a dialogue between the Ministry and governments of federate-states and municipalities, thus giving more capillarity to the formulation process of foreign policy." *Itamaraty* has also set up "regional offices or local antennas in various federate-states."[124] In Brazil, all municipal governments with international structures (as shown below) deal with bilateral and multilateral international cooperation, which is the core area of the Brazilian paradiplomatic agenda.[125]

In 2011, around 29 municipalities within Brazilian cities had formal paradiplomatic structures.[126] The structures and functions developed by the municipalities reflect Brazil's concept of paradiplomacy that defines the characteristics of subnational municipal international relations in the South.

In Brazilian municipal governments, the local authorities demonstrate a considerable degree of responsibility in the city's negotiation of cooperation agreements. It is the municipal authorities who themselves accept or reject cooperation proposals from foreign municipalities or subnational entities. Many municipal international relations structures also deal with raising funds from international agencies, such as the World Bank, International Monetary Fund or Fonplata. In the South, "fund-raising is frequently the main *raison d'être* of municipal foreign policy and one of the greatest motivations for a municipal government's decision to establish an international relations structure."[127]

The multilateral agencies like the World Bank have begun to directly deal with subnational governments to negotiate loans and cooperation agreements.

The strategies that are devised are increasingly centred on economically and technically strengthening non-central governments. São Paulo and Porto Alegre were the first cities and Rio Grande do Sul and Minas Gerais, the first states, to take the opportunities offered in order to increase the availability of resources for local development.[128] A team of experts was put into place, who hold expertise in drafting proposals and handling negotiations with international agencies. The municipal administration designs the development projects for which these experts seek financing and investment from foreign countries. Such projects or initiatives are often recommended by international agencies to the local authorities for specific areas. After the political agreement is formalised, the city council's technical team prepares the proposal for submission in accordance with the agency's directives, although always under the Brazilian federal government's strict supervision.

Such policies of international development agencies had defined Brazilian paradiplomacy. In addition, the transnational city networks and organisations supported by international organisations, such as the UN-Habitat Programme, UNDP or EU's European Commission played an important role in Brazil's paradiplomatic affairs.[129] Besides, some Brazilian mayors gained global recognition through the international cities' movement. At the same time, some Brazilian mayors and other municipal authorities became active members of various international organisations of cities and local authorities and of various international networks. The most important network, in terms of its size and impact, is the bi-regional URB-AL programme of the European Union, which was launched in 1995 and is currently in its third phase. The URB-AL gives support to the cooperation between the local governments of the European Union and Latin America by "forming thematic networks concerning concrete urban policies in which several multilateral projects are organised among multiple European and Latin American participants."[130] The participants themselves, along with the European Commission, fund these projects, but it is exclusively "the participating local governments that propose, manage and implement them. URB-AL has had considerable impact, both qualitatively through its innovative identification and formulation mechanisms for joint projects in each network. The programme, with nearly 1.8 million beneficiaries, is made up of 20 cooperation projects implemented in 74 Latin American territories and by an Office of Coordination and Orientation

(OCO)."[131] Within the framework of the URB-AL III, "131 local public policies have been generated or strengthened that contribute to fostering social cohesion in more than 500 Latin American municipalities."[132] Brazilian municipal governments have participated in all the theme-based networks and have organised various projects. Brazil also conducted "two thematic networks on Network 9 on 'Local Financing and Participatory Budget', which was led by Porto Alegre."[133] The other one was on Network 10 on the 'Fight against Urban Poverty' led by São Paulo.[134]

The networks in which Brazilian municipal governments participate most actively and which have fairly precise objectives are the "International Association of Educating Cities, the International Centre for Strategic Urban Development, which is responsible for the international dissemination of the strategic plan devised by the city of Barcelona and the International Council for Local Environmental Initiatives (ICLEI)."[135] The Brazilian paradiplomacy attained worldwide recognition when the Brazilian municipal governments attended the Habitat II conference or 'City Summit' in Istanbul in 1996.[136] The delegation from Brazilian municipal governments in the Summit and the Assembly of Cities that was held parallel to the summit strengthened its development of international municipal strategies. This enabled the municipal governments to increase their involvement in the key political processes of the international local governments' movement, such as the establishment of a single world organisation of local governments through the merger of the two main existing organisations (IULA and FMCU-UTO), the search for a forum in the United Nations System and specifically, in the UN-HABITAT Programme, where "local governments could participate and the promulgation of a universal standard on local autonomy and decentralisation."[137]

The participation of municipal governments and local authorities in the structural as well as procedural matters of municipal foreign interaction has largely shaped the way subnational governments organised their paradiplomacy in Brazil. The subnational governments formed strategies and internationalised their projects to attain global recognition on a large scale. First, as mentioned before, international cooperation and participation in city networks was seen as the core of Brazilian paradiplomacy. Second, the international dissemination of the best practices, whether by the UN-Habitat or other agencies, was soon identified as a powerful channel for city-marketing. Third, Brazilian mayors discovered that international activism could also have a political impact, which could be used domestically. The mayor of São Paulo, Marta Suplicy, led an intense campaign of international contacts waged by the city council's Municipal Secretariat of International Relations in 2004 and also managed to become one of the first three co-presidents of the UCLG in 2004. Tarso Genro, the mayor of Porto Alegre and more recently, Eloi Pietá, the mayor of Guarulhos, have been among Brazil's most internationally active mayors.[138]

Within Brazilian paradiplomacy, economic cooperation and trade promotion is an area incorporated within federated states rather than the municipal governments. In this sense, the municipal governments do not directly indulge in economic cooperation, but attract foreign investments through city-marketing. City-marketing or the creation of a 'city brand' is one of the major aspects of the internationalisation strategy of local governments and an indispensable tool of municipal foreign policy. For instance, Rio de Janeiro and São Paulo, with their image as 'global cities' in terms of connectivity, infrastructure development, human resources and tourist attractions, have invited potential foreign partners to set up large businesses in the cities. Furthermore, the 'Curitiba model' of town planning, formed in 1960 with the collaboration of the Institute of Research and Town Planning of Curitiba (*Instituto de Pesquisa e Planejamento Urbano de Curitiba*), has been used together with the multicultural origins of the city's population to create an internationally attractive city image. The City Council refers to Curitiba city as the "Brazilian capital of multiculturality."[139]

Another example is the 'image-building strategy' of Porto Alegre, which brands itself as a 'global solidarity city' or 'democracy network city'. The city is in association with the World Social Forum (WSF) and has hosted the first (2001), second (2002), third (2003) and fifth (2005) editions of the WSF. The international dissemination of Porto Alegre's Participatory Budgeting is its strong asset in promoting cooperation.[140] The international activism of Brazilian cities and municipalities through the country's formal structures and municipal foreign policy has set an example for developing countries to make the practice of paradiplomacy effectual in their foreign policy.

Brazil has not institutionalised paradiplomacy within its constitutional framework, yet its federated states and municipalities have managed to strengthen their presence in international relations. Similarly, within India, there is no constitutional mandate or a separate institution to carry out paradiplomatic activities. Although Indian states and cities, during the past decades, have conducted sister-city exchanges, their presence is very limited when it comes to foreign interactions at international platforms. This is due to lack of paradiplomatic structures at the state and local level. In the States Division within the MEA, there seems to be no specific development strategy that can smoothly carry out city-to-city diplomacy at the subnational level. Within Brazil, cities participate in various international organisations through formal structures and functions. Cities like São Paulo and Rio de Janeiro have successfully hosted multilateral summits and seminars. Such activities have helped Brazilian cities build an international image.

The paradiplomatic structures have enabled the active participation of Brazilian municipal entities in urban issues in various international organisations like the FNP and UN-Habitat II. Such initiatives have demonstrated the international activism of Brazilian mayors and local authorities. Another important aspect that India needs to learn from Brazilian paradiplomacy and China's urban diplomacy is their consistent attempts at obtaining regional integration through paradiplomatic activities. Despite their cross-border conflicts and geographic rivalries, China's BRI initiative and Brazil's Mercosur have strengthened their regional and economic cooperation by involving cities and subnational entities in sub-regional organisations. In the case of India, this can only be possible if paradiplomacy is institutionalised at the local level within Indian states and cities. The concluding chapter prescribes a model of paradiplomatic structures within India's foreign policy framework.

Notes

1. Britannica, "Mao and the Chinese Communist Party," https://www.britannica.com/, https://www.britannica.com/biography/Mao-Zedong/Mao-and-the-Chinese-Communist-Party.
2. Dominik Mierzejewski, "Channelling Foreign Policy through Local Activities in China: City of Guangzhou - Case Study," in *Paradiplomacy in Asia: Case Studies of China, India and Russia* (Poland: Lodz University Press, 2018).
3. Li Xinyu Li Xiaolin, *Urban Diplomacy: Theory and Practice* (China: Social Science Academic Press, 2016).

4. www.gov.cn, "Constitution of the People's Republic of China," The People's Republic of China, http://english.www.gov.cn/archive/lawsregulations/201911/20/content_WS5ed8856ec6d0b3f0e9499913.html.
5. Ibid.
6. Britannica, "Constitutional Framework," https://www.britannica.com/, https://www.britannica.com/place/China/Constitutional-framework.
7. Li Xiaolin, *Urban Diplomacy: Theory and Practice.*
8. There are five levels of local governments in China—Province, autonomous region, municipality and special administrative region.
9. Li Xiaolin, *Urban Diplomacy: Theory and Practice.*
10. Ibid.
11. Ibid.
12. chinatoday.com, "The Communist Party of China (CPC, CCP)," China Information and Sources, http://www.chinatoday.com/org/cpc/.
13. Li Xiaolin, *Urban Diplomacy: Theory and Practice.*
14. Ibid.
15. CPAFFC, "The Chinese People's Association for Friendship with Foreign Countries (CPAFFC)," www.cpaffc.org.cn/, https://cpaffc.org.cn/index/xiehui/xiehui_list/cate/11/lang/2.html.
16. Li Xiaolin, *Urban Diplomacy: Theory and Practice.*
17. Ibid.
18. Ibid.
19. ChinaDaily, "Xi: There Is No Gene for Invasion in Our Blood," China Daily USA, http://usa.chinadaily.com.cn/china/2014-05/16/content_17511170.htm.
20. "This Day, That Year: June 24".
21. Wang Yanqi, "Chinese City Diplomacy Should Integrate Resources to Serve the Country's Overall Interest," Shanghai Forum, https://shanghaiforum.fudan.edu.cn/_upload/article/files/72/67/b1c5c95043e8b02f0a89eb395770/9deb0f48-9f7c-4f89-9601-0106eb3cebf7.pdf.
22. Ibid.
23. MOFA, "Joint Communique of the Government of Japan and the Government of the People's Republic of China," ed. Ministry of Foreign Affairs of Japan (Japan: MOFA, 1972).
24. ChinaDaily, "This Day, That Year: June 24".
25. Li Xiaolin, *Urban Diplomacy: Theory and Practice.*
26. Ibid.
27. Ibid.
28. ChinaDaily, "This Day, That Year: June 24".
29. Li Xiaolin, *Urban Diplomacy: Theory and Practice.*
30. Ibid.

31. Ibid.
32. Ibid.
33. Elizabeth K. Pitts, "Chinese Foreign Relations in a Local Setting : The Sister City Program of the People's Republic of China" (The Hong Kong University of Science and Technology, 1996).
34. IULA, "Iula Promotes Democratic Local Governments Worldwide".
35. Li Xiaolin, *Urban Diplomacy: Theory and Practice.*
36. Zhan Lisheng, "Mayors and Urban Officials Converge in Guangzhou," China Daily, http://www.chinadaily.com.cn/cndy/2009-11/12/content_8954613.htm.
37. Xinhuanet.com, "The Report Analyzes China's "Urban Diplomacy": Shifting from Focusing on Gain to Actively Giving," China News Network, http://www.xinhuanet.com/politics/2016-03/17/c_128808031.htm.
38. Ibid.
39. Li Xiaolin, *Urban Diplomacy: Theory and Practice.*
40. Ibid.
41. Xinhuanet.com, "The Report Analyzes China's "Urban Diplomacy": Shifting from Focusing on Gain to Actively Giving".
42. Ibid.
43. CPAFFC, "The Chinese People's Association for Friendship with Foreign Countries (CPAFFC)".
44. Li Xiaolin, *Urban Diplomacy: Theory and Practice.*
45. Ibid.
46. Ibid.
47. Ibid.
48. Ibid.
49. Olympic.org, "Beijing 2008," https://www.olympic.org/beijing-2008.
50. ChinaBriefing, "Expo Shanghai 2010," https://www.china-briefing.com, https://www.china-briefing.com/news/expo/.
51. ChinaDaily, "Shanghai Free Trade Zone Makes Impressive Progress over 7 Years," China Daily, https://www.prnewswire.com/news-releases/shanghai-free-trade-zone-makes-impressive-progress-over-7-years-301158556.html.
52. Ibid.
53. Li Xiaolin, *Urban Diplomacy: Theory and Practice.*
54. Ibid.
55. Embassy of the People's Republic of China, "Speech by Premier Wen Jiabao of the State Council of the People's Republic of China at the Japanese Diet," news release, 2007, http://lk.china-embassy.org/eng/zgxw/t311107.htm.
56. CGTN, "China-Japan Ties: Ancient Temple in Japan Witnesses Centuries of Exchanges," https://news.cgtn.com/, https://news.cgtn.com/news/7a4d7a4d774d4464776c6d636a4e6e62684a4856/index.html.

57. China, "Speech by Premier Wen Jiabao of the State Council of the People's Republic of China at the Japanese Diet."
58. Ibid.
59. Ibid.
60. BBC, "Why Narendra Modi's First China Stop Is Xian," https://www.bbc.com/, https://www.bbc.com/news/world-asia-china-32732402.
61. Ibid.
62. Ibid.
63. Ibid.
64. Liu Jianfei, "Major-Country Diplomacy with Chinese Characteristics Reflects Trends of the Times," *China International Studies* (2017), https://heinonline.org/HOL/LandingPage?handle=hein.journals/chintersd64&div=5&id=&page=.
65. FMPRC, "Study and Implement Xi Jinping Thought on Diplomacy Conscientiously and Break New Ground in Major-Country Diplomacy with Chinese Characteristics," www.fmprc.gov.cn, https://www.fmprc.gov.cn/mfa_eng/zxxx_662805/t1799305.shtml.
66. Li Xiaolin, *Urban Diplomacy: Theory and Practice.*
67. Ibid.
68. NDRC, "Vision and Actions on Jointly Building Silk Road Economic Belt and 21st-Century Maritime Silk Road," news release, 2015, https://en.ndrc.gov.cn/newsrelease_8232/201503/t20150330_1193900.html.
69. Huping Shang, *The Belth and Road Initiative: Key Concepts* (Peking University Press: Springer, 2019).
70. NDRC, "Vision and Actions on Jointly Building Silk Road Economic Belt and 21st-Century Maritime Silk Road."
71. Ibid.
72. Ibid.
73. Ibid.
74. Ibid.
75. Ibid.
76. Ibid.
77. Li Xiaolin, *Urban Diplomacy: Theory and Practice.*
78. Ibid.
79. Ibid.
80. Ibid.
81. UCLG-ASPAC, "21st-Century Maritime Cooperation Committee," https://uclg-aspac.org/, https://uclg-aspac.org/en/the-21st-century-maritime-cooperation-committee/.

82. chinacopyrightandmedia.wordpress.com, "Communiqué of the Fifth Plenary Meeting of the 18th Central Committee of the Chinese Communist Party," China Copyright and Media, https://chinacopyrightandmedia.wordpress.com/2015/10/29/communique-of-the-fifth-plenary-meeting-of-the-18th-central-committee-of-the-chinese-communist-party/.
83. Li Xiaolin, *Urban Diplomacy: Theory and Practice.*
84. Xinhuanet.com, "Pan-Beibu Gulf Economic Cooperation Forum to Be Held in October," http://www.xinhuanet.com/, http://www.xinhuanet.com/english/2020-09/16/c_139372899.htm.
85. ASEAN, "Asean Mekong Basin Development Cooperation", https://asean.org/, https://asean.org/asean-economic-community/asean-mekong-basin-development-cooperation-ambdc/overview/.
86. Li Xiaolin, *Urban Diplomacy: Theory and Practice.*
87. Ibid.
88. Ibid.
89. ECLAC-UN, "Brazil—Political and Electoral System," United Nations Economic Commission for Latin America and the Caribbean, https://oig.cepal.org/en/countries/7/system.
90. Ibid.
91. Carlos R. S. Milani, "International Relations and the Paradiplomacy of Brazilian Cities: Crafting the Concept of Local International Management," *Brazilian Administration Review* (2011).
92. Marcos Napolitano, "The Brazilian Military Regime, 1964–1985," *Latin American History* (2018), https://oxfordre.com/latinamericanhistory/view/10.1093/acrefore/9780199366439.001.0001/acrefore-9780199366439-e-413.
93. Ibid.
94. Governo do Brasil, "Brazil's Democratic Constitution of 1988 Was Built by Society," https://www.gov.br/pt-br, http://www.brazil.gov.br/about-brazil/news/2018/11/brazils-democratic-constitution-of-1988-was-built-by-society#:~:text=Arising%20from%20intense%20popular%20outcry,20%20months%20in%20the%20National.
95. Milani, "International Relations and the Paradiplomacy of Brazilian Cities: Crafting the Concept of Local International Management."
96. Ibid.
97. Alexandre Figueiredo, "Paradiplomacy and National Development," VERMELHO, https://vermelho.org.br/internacional/.
98. WIPO, "Constituição Da República Federativa Do Brasil De 1988 Incluindo Reformas De 1992, 1993, 1994, 1995, 1996," (2008), https://www.wipo.int/edocs/lexdocs/laws/en/br/br117en.pdf.
99. Ibid.

100. Milani, "International Relations and the Paradiplomacy of Brazilian Cities: Crafting the Concept of Local International Management."
101. Mark Amen, "Paradiplomacy in the Developing World: The Case of Brazil," in *Cities and Global Governance: New Sites for International Relations*, ed. Monica Salomon (England: Ashgate Publishing Limited, 2011).
102. Ibid., p. 59.
103. Ibid.
104. Ibid., p. 50.
105. Ibid., p. 51.
106. Ibid., p. 52.
107. Agência Câmara de Notícias, "Pec Allows State and Municipality to Make External Agreement," news release, 2005, https://www.camara.leg.br/noticias/78558-pec-permite-a-estado-e-municipio-fazerem-acordo-externo/.
108. Milani, "International Relations and the Paradiplomacy of Brazilian Cities: Crafting the Concept of Local International Management."
109. CNM, "Quem Somos," Confederação Nacional de Municípios, https://www.cnm.org.br/institucional/conhecaacnm.
110. FNP, "Join," Frente Nacional de Prefeitos, https://www.fnp.org.br/filie-se.
111. Milani, "International Relations and the Paradiplomacy of Brazilian Cities: Crafting the Concept of Local International Management," p. 4.
112. Figueiredo, "Paradiplomacy and National Development".
113. Mercociudades, "Ciudades Miembros," https://mercociudades.org/.
114. Ibid.
115. Milani, "International Relations and the Paradiplomacy of Brazilian Cities: Crafting the Concept of Local International Management."
116. Mark Amen, "Paradiplomacy in the Developing World: The Case of Brazil," p. 60.
117. Boaventura de Sousa Santos, "Participatory Budgeting in Porto Alegre: Toward a Redistributive Democracy," *Politics & Society* 26, no. 4 (1998), https://www.ssc.wisc.edu/~wright/santosweb.html.
118. Mark Amen, "Paradiplomacy in the Developing World: The Case of Brazil."
119. Ibid., p. 54.
120. Ibid.
121. Ibid.
122. Ibid.
123. Ibid.
124. Milani, "International Relations and the Paradiplomacy of Brazilian Cities: Crafting the Concept of Local International Management."
125. Mark Amen, "Paradiplomacy in the Developing World: The Case of Brazil."

126. Milani, "International Relations and the Paradiplomacy of Brazilian Cities: Crafting the Concept of Local International Management," p. 8.
127. Mark Amen, "Paradiplomacy in the Developing World: The Case of Brazil," p. 55.
128. Ibid.
129. Ibid., p. 55.
130. Observatorio, "Programme Urb-Al Iii," https://www.observ-ocd.org/en/programme-urb-al-iii.
131. Ibid.
132. Ibid.
133. Santos, "Participatory Budgeting in Porto Alegre: Toward a Redistributive Democracy".
134. URB-AL, "Poverty as a Violation of Human Rights" (paper presented at the International Conference Network 10—Fight Against Urban Poverty, São Paulo, 2004).
135. Mark Amen, "Paradiplomacy in the Developing World: The Case of Brazil," p. 56.
136. UN, "City Summit" (paper presented at the United Nations Conference on Human Settlements (Habitat II), Istanbul, 1996).
137. Mark Amen, "Paradiplomacy in the Developing World: The Case of Brazil," p. 57.
138. Ibid.
139. Ibid., p. 58.
140. Santos, "Participatory Budgeting in Porto Alegre: Toward a Redistributive Democracy".

7

Conclusion

In the preceding chapters, an attempt has been made to study the practice of paradiplomacy in India's diplomatic endeavours. After studying the trend, it can be argued that paradiplomacy, as a practice, is yet to gain a foothold in India's mainstream diplomatic agendas. Although the concept has attracted global attention, especially in academic circles, it is yet to be recognised and practiced by the majority of countries. The diplomatic initiatives independently carried out by subnational governments still remain under the shadow of the federal government's prerogative due to the prevalent tradition of the nation-state as the primary international actors. It will take a few more years for the paradiplomacy concept and its practice to acquire space in the national mainstream agenda.

One needs to acknowledge that paradiplomacy is not a one-dimensional concept, but a multi-layered term. The four stages of paradiplomacy discussed in the second chapter bring to the fore, the role of subnational actors, which is prevalent mostly in federal polities, such as Canada, Germany, Belgium, Switzerland, Australia and the US, as well as some unitary polities like Spain and France. The study concludes that the practice of paradiplomacy does not challenge the 'nation-states' status as primary actors and units of analysis; however, it changes the nature and course of interaction between the states. The chapter also established the fact that paradiplomacy is simply an extension of modern diplomatic activities and not a different concept altogether.

In the third chapter, the inception of paradiplomacy and its practice in ancient cities as well as modern cities in the 20th century has been analysed. During the late 20th century, globalisation caused internationalisation of domestic affairs that broadened the practice of paradiplomacy. The diplomatic initiatives of provinces like Quebec and states like California laid the foundations for paradiplomacy as a diplomatic strategy among subnational governments. Paradiplomacy achieved a breakthrough in the 21st century due to its notable practices in the sub-states of Argentina, Brazil, Chile, China, Japan, India, Mexico, Russia and South Africa. The third chapter, by delving into history, demonstrates that paradiplomacy is not a new phenomenon; rather, it evolved over centuries. The practice of paradiplomacy in economic, cultural and environmental domains gained limelight in the 21st century. The current global trend indicates that cities are the new actors in the international arena and their presence cannot be overlooked.

Cities are the backbone of the economic growth of a country. Due to increasing foreign interactions and economic activities, cities and states have surpassed countries in generating GDP. The available data suggests that cities are becoming the fulcrum of the national economy and it is expected that it would facilitate their paradiplomatic activities in global affairs. "Due to the sheer volume of economic activity and concentrated resource usage over which they have at least some degree of jurisdiction, cities are well-positioned to pursue agendas of urban metabolic efficiency and generate meaningful impact independent of nation-states and forums of subnational governments that focuses on issues ranging from sustainable development to culture and education and urban development."[1] Around 200 inter-city networks are currently jointly working to grapple with challenges, such as migration and climate change.

The fourth and fifth chapters focused on the practice of paradiplomacy in developing countries like India. Cities like Mumbai and Delhi have found their place in the world's top 100 economies. Indian cities and states have strengthened their foreign interactions through sister agreements, smart city initiatives and business partnerships. India's outlook towards the states' involvement in foreign relations has implied that paradiplomacy would be a new dimension in India's foreign policy. Currently, India has approximately 100 sister-city and sister-state agreements with foreign cities and provinces. The MEA has created the States Division for promoting trade and investments and cultural diplomacy. The Modi government has laid emphasis on 'cooperative federalism' and further increasing the states' influence in India's foreign policy. However, the states' and cities' foreign interactions are mostly based on economic cooperation. The chapter also concluded that paradiplomacy is an economic compulsion rather than a diplomatic offshoot. The chapter delved into the foreign interactions of Indian states and cities in the pre-reform period (before 1990) and post-reform period. It examined how the practice of paradiplomacy has accelerated India's economic growth and its global connectivity.

Given that paradiplomacy as a formal activity in India is still in its infancy, the sixth chapter highlights the important takeaways for India from paradiplomatic practices in other countries like China and Brazil. This chapter points out that there are various strategic and security issues where the central government is required to consult Indian states, regarding decisions involving relations with neighbouring countries. After studying China's approach to paradiplomacy, the chapter highlights that India is yet to develop its paradiplomatic policies that can determine its role in regional and economic integration. Moreover, Brazil's Municipal Foreign Policy suggests that India needs a proper mandate and paradiplomatic structures to institutionalise paradiplomacy at the state and local level. Due to lack of consensus between the states and the centre in many areas, the prospects of paradiplomacy seem low in India.

Limitations of Paradiplomacy in India

Although India's practice of paradiplomacy shows a phenomenal growth within a decade of its inception in 2013, a separate institutional apparatus to deal with such activities is still in its infancy. India seems to be on a learning curve to adopt paradiplomacy in letter and spirit in its foreign policy making. Various measures and policy initiatives undertaken by Narendra Modi have, however, set the pace for paradiplomacy in India. It is also discernible from the discussion in Chapter 5 that the initiatives undertaken by the union government are largely centred on economic cooperation, twinning agreements and cultural diplomacy. Happymon Jacob, in an article, argues that "such efforts are largely ad hoc and functionalist in nature rather than being holistic and structurally transformative."[2]

In terms of driving urban development and economic growth, the central government has emphasised on the 'Double Engine *Sarkaar*', which means a political party that is elected at the central level as well as the state level. Modi, during his speech in February 2023 at the launch of multiple development initiatives in Belgavi, Karnataka, has stated that, "The double-engine government is a guarantee for fast-paced development."[3] But, on the other hand, the slogan has raised various debates on the efficacy of federalism in India in a double engine government. These debates are largely centred on the governance structure being centralised, which seems to be one of the major concerns of a double engine government. Nonetheless, the paradiplomatic practices facilitated by the double engine government has gradually increased Ease of Doing Business and foreign investment in Karnataka. Such instances imply how the double engine government can be integrated with India's quasi-federal structure. Yet, it remains to be seen how the central government would incorporate the implications of a double-engine government within competitive and cooperative federalism.

The Indian model of federalism poses certain issues that have impeded Indian states' participation in foreign policy matters, such as the Seventh Schedule of the Constitution of India. Article 246 of the Constitution of India divides legislative powers into three lists: Union List, State List and Concurrent List. According to the Union List, the union government has exclusive authority to "conduct foreign relations, diplomatic, consular and trade representation, participation in international conferences and UN, entering into treaties and agreements, inter-state trade and commerce etc."[4] Thus, state governments have limited authority to conduct external relations. Most of the twinning and sister-city agreements (discussed in Chapter 5) are concluded by the MEA; the role of the state governments is actually confined to the facilitation of foreign visits and programmes. Although the state governments are consulted by the MEA before the signing of agreements, they have minimal influence in foreign policy matters. However, during the 1990s, for the structural adjustments of the Indian economy, this scenario changed and opened new possibilities for the states to participate in international economic activities. Despite this, the Constitution of India does not bestow on the state governments any specific role or importance in India's foreign policy conduct, as the subject is a constitutional prerogative of the union government.

The government's significant approach towards paradiplomatic practices since 2014, such as sister-city agreements, vibrant summits and the creation of the 'States Division' encouraged the states to participate in foreign policy matters. The States Division has facilitated various programmes and foreign visits (Table 5.3). The highest number of sister-city agreements have been concluded under the Modi government. Although Modi has laid great emphasis on cooperative and competitive federalism, there is still a lack of consensus between the union government and state governments in the area of foreign policy. There are various cases where the Centre has denied the foreign visits of some chief ministers. For instance, the chief minister of Delhi, Arvind Kejriwal, was not given political clearance to attend the World Cities Summit organised in July 2019.[5] Later, in October 2021, the chief minister of West Bengal, Mamta Banerjee, was not permitted by the MEA to attend the World Peace Conference held in Rome.[6] Banerjee was also denied a visit to Nepal, where she was invited by the prime minister of Nepal, Sher Bahadur Deuba, to attend the annual conference of his party.[7] The Centre's denial of permission for the foreign visits of chief ministers is largely attributed to the political tensions and differences between the regional parties and the central government. Besides, there is no dedicated institutional apparatus with a proper channel of coordination at the local level. For instance, the States Division established by the MEA is a central government body that precludes any state-level representatives. The States Division is only empowered to enhance international cooperation in economic activities. With regard to strategic issues, the decision-making authority absolutely lies with the central government. There are various instances where the States Division has been curbed/stopped from dealing with security-related agreements or cooperation. In fact, the MEA has clarified that the Division would not address disputes pertaining to policy, such as the Teesta accord between Bangladesh and West Bengal and issues involving Sri Lanka and Tamil Nadu. However, during the negotiations on the Sir Creek dispute, the then chief minister of Gujarat, Narendra Modi, wrote a letter to Prime Minister Manmohan Singh, cautioning on the adverse effects of handing over Sir Creek to Pakistan without consulting Gujarat.[8] This instance implies that it is necessary for the bordering states to be consulted while entering into any agreement with a neighbouring country. Such instances indicate that cooperative and competitive federalism seem ineffective, owing to the lack of consensus in the union government and between the state and union governments.

Furthermore, the Inter-State Council (ISC), created to act as an intermediary institution between the centre and the states, also seems ineffective in building a clear consensus. The ISC is "chaired by the Prime Minister and is formed of Chief Ministers as well as some Cabinet Ministers, but no other state representatives."[9] Jacob has suggested that the government should focus on reinforcing the existing coordination mechanism in institutions like the Inter-State Council and National Development Council. There should be collaboration and cooperation in centre-state relations, by involving the state ministers and local authorities in the decision-making process. There should also be provisions in the case of bordering states sharing international boundaries. For instance, India's policy towards China has repercussions on Arunachal Pradesh, Sikkim, Ladakh and Jammu and Kashmir. Its dealings with Pakistan have definite repercussions on the bordering states like Gujarat, Rajasthan, Jammu and Kashmir and Punjab. India's relations with Bangladesh have direct implications for West Bengal, Assam, Meghalaya, Mizoram and Tripura. Myanmar-India relations equally affect Nagaland, Mizoram, Manipur and Arunachal Pradesh due to their proximity. Lastly, India's policy towards Nepal has repercussions for Bihar, Uttarakhand, Sikkim, Uttar Pradesh and West Bengal. Thus, conducting effective diplomacy with the neighbouring countries largely depends on the coordination between the respective state governments and the Union government.

However, the border disputes with neighbours and illegal immigration, illicit drug and human trafficking and arms smuggling and insurgency rampant in these states have hindered the smooth engagement of all parties concerned. The north-eastern region is considered as India's gateway to the ASEAN. But lack of stringent border management and inadequate connectivity of infrastructure have constrained the north-eastern states' effective engagement in India's neighbourhood policy. However, the Modi government, under the vision of the Act East Policy, has attempted to involve them. The government should also emphasise on strengthening paradiplomatic practices in BIMARU states that comprise Bihar, Madhya Pradesh, Rajasthan, and Uttar Pradesh. These states have shown slower economic development in the region compared to the other Indian states. Although the government has facilitated various summits in these states to attract foreign investments, they require more paradiplomatic interactions to increase their economic engagement in terms of building railway projects, road infrastructure, development of IT parks, healthcare systems and tourism. In 2021, the Ministry of Tourism organised a Buddhist Circuit Train—a route that encompasses the holy sites of Gautam Buddha, such as his birthplace in Lumbini situated in Nepal and Bodh Gaya in Bihar, where he attained enlightenment.[10] In Uttar Pradesh, the Buddha presented his first sermon in Sarnath and Kushinagar was his final departure site. The prominent Buddhist sites like Bodh Gaya, Nalanda, Rajgir, Vaishali, Sarnath, Shravasti, Kushinagar, Kaushambi, Sankisa and Kapilavastu attract six percent of the foreign tourists.[11] The Ministry of Tourism has been aggressively promoting India as a Buddhist destination in countries like Vietnam, Thailand, Japan, South Korea and Sri Lanka.

Furthermore, keeping in mind the tensions between India and Pakistan, a Punjab-to-Punjab (Indian Punjab and Pakistan Punjab) cooperation was established across national boundaries through various joint initiatives. In 2012, both the governments established "an integrated check post at the village of Attari, followed by exchanges and agreements on the promotion of culture, education, science and economics in subsequent years."[12]

During the time of the pandemic, India witnessed the highest surge in COVID-19 cases during the second wave in Delhi, Mumbai, Bangalore, Chennai and Kolkata. Arvind Kejriwal, the chief minister of Delhi, placed global tenders with Johnson & Johnson, Moderna and Pfizer, but the "US pharmaceutical firms refused to sell their coronavirus vaccines directly to the national capital as they only deal with the centre."[13] This led to a massive shortage of supply of vaccine doses in the country, causing Delhi to shut down its vaccination centres for the 18-44 age category.[14]

Such instances highlight the necessity of a robust mechanism to integrate the states in foreign policy matters. Due to lack of specialised institutions and standard provisions that can facilitate the paradiplomatic activities, most of the sister-city agreements are not annually reviewed to evaluate their performance. Thus, for the lack of institutional structure and adequate procedure, the future of paradiplomacy seems uncertain. India needs to institutionalise paradiplomacy with a proper mandate within its foreign policy establishment. This study, at the end, proposes an institutional framework for streamlining paradiplomacy in India.

Paradiplomacy, as a diplomatic activity, has never been homogeneous among countries due to divergence in government structures. Initially, the concept of paradiplomacy was mainly suited to federal structures and its practice was confined to the western countries. Eventually, it gained recognition and many countries attempted to accommodate paradiplomacy. For instance, India, despite its constitutional provisions and quasi-federal structure, is trying to empower local governments and cities to undertake twinning and economic cooperation agreements with foreign cities and states. Similarly, China implemented paradiplomacy under the name of 'China's Urban Diplomacy' through the involvement of provinces and cities in the BRI to strengthen its regional integration strategy. China has engaged its provinces and cities in promoting economic, cultural and social development, but their role is minimal. China's paradiplomacy seems to act as a catalyst for China's economic reforms and globalisation policy. This indicates that China's urban diplomacy may be distinct from the original concept of paradiplomacy.

Another instance is Russia's paradiplomacy in the north that has become a vital strategy in Russia's Arctic policy. The Russian Federation consists of 89 constituent units, also referred to as 'subjects of Federation'. They are divided into six different types—republics, territories, regions, federal cities, autonomous areas and autonomous regions.[15] These constituent units have exclusive powers to enter into international agreements with foreign countries with the consent of the federation.[16] Russia's subnational actors in the Arctic include the AZRF (Arctic Zone of the Russian Federation) regions and municipalities that consists of the Murmansk Region, Nenets Autonomous District, the Chukotka Autonomous District, Yamalo-Nenets Autonomous District, the Republic of Karelia, the Komi Republic, the Republic of Sakha (Yakutia), Krasnoyarsk Region and Arkhangelsk Region. Russia's conduct of paradiplomatic activities in Arctic affairs through its subnational actors has subsequently influenced Russia's position in foreign policy matters and international treaties of the Arctic region.

Russia's Arctic policy involves the development of the northern sea route as a shipping channel and using the seas as a transportation system.[17] Russia claims a part of the Arctic continental shelf with an intent to utilise its untapped oil, natural gas and other resources and further develop the Arctic Zone.[18] Paradiplomacy has undoubtedly been instrumental in solving problems with respect to "Russia's relations with neighbouring countries and in this regard, has become an important integrative function."[19] Russia's Arctic paradiplomacy has served as a crucial strategy in shaping Russia's Arctic foreign policy.

From all these instances, it can be assumed that paradiplomacy does not have a uniform definition. Moreover, the concept of paradiplomacy is interdisciplinary in its approach and accordingly, each country defines paradiplomacy in its own context. Moreover, the attributes of paradiplomacy are dynamic and therefore, the contextual variance of paradiplomacy would remain.

Suggestions and Recommendations

Considering the limitations, an attempt is made to suggest a toolkit or model that would streamline the role of the Indian states and cities in foreign policy making. The model suggested here prescribes a new process for the effective implementation of paradiplomacy in India at the state and local level. Besides, there are various policy recommendations which can be implemented to involve the states and cities in foreign policy matters more effectively.

Figure 7.1: Institutional Framework of Paradiplomacy in India

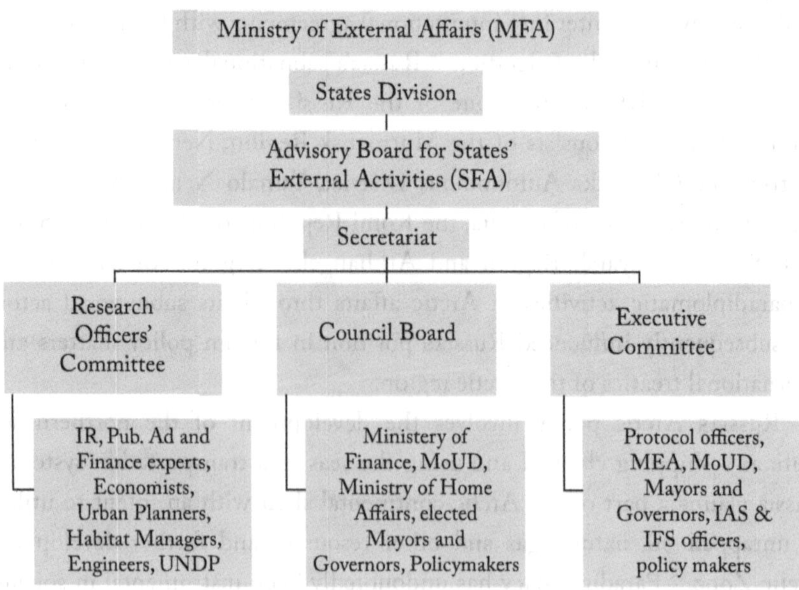

It is a prerequisite for the government to develop a proper channel of coordination where the states can carry out external activities in certain areas, such as trade, investment and cultural exchanges. The suggested model may help further the process of Indian paradiplomacy to institutionalise and facilitate the states to realise their potential to contribute constructively and strengthen India's foreign policy.

Figure 7.2: The Process of SEA Advisory Board

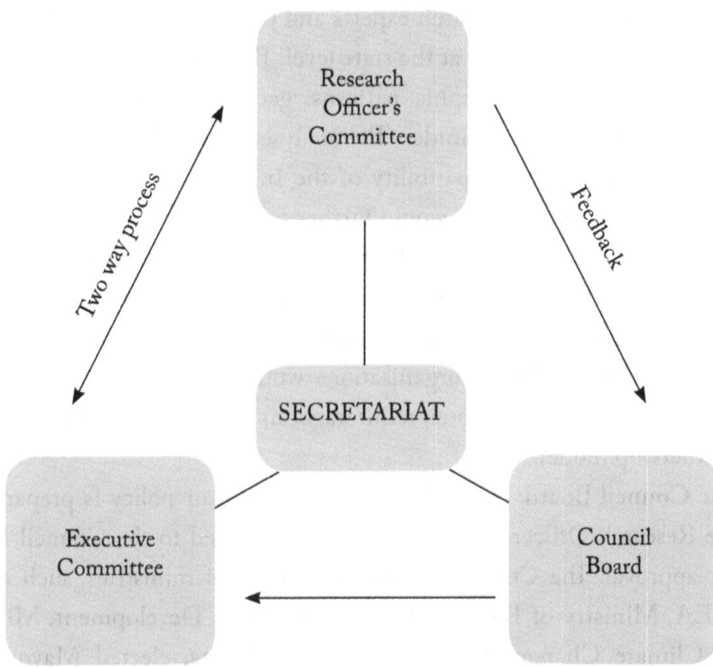

At the outset, the model proposes the union government to establish a Central Advisory Board as the apex body for paradiplomatic activities in every state. The advisory board may be named as the 'States' External Activities (SEA)', functioning under the 'States Division' created by the MEA. The advisory board would be assisted by a secretariat that comprises three divisions, which are: (1) Research Officers' Committee; (2) Council Board; and (3) Executive Committee. Apart from the Council Board, the officers and experts of the other two divisions are appointed by the Prime Minister Office

(PMO) in consultation with the MEA. Figure 7.2 explains the process of the SEA for effective functioning as given below:

1. **The Research Officers' Committee:** With the increasing number of sister-city tie-ups and cultural exchanges across the nation, it is required for states to conduct research analysis and statistical surveys at the grassroot level. The purpose of the Research Officers' Committee is to analyse the demands of the city inhabitants and study urban agglomerations and socio-economic development in different cities. Each city or region would have its own team of research experts and planners, which shall report to the committee, operating at the state level. The aim is to study these cities based on their demographic patterns, geographic diversity, economic activities and cultural attitudes. The analysis would allow the committee to comprehend the compatibility of the Indian states and cities with a foreign city/province. This would further facilitate city-to-city diplomacy and business opportunities with other countries. The committee includes experts on international relations, public administration, economics, finance, urban planners, habitat managers, engineers and organisations like the UNDP. Private organisations would also play a major role in city development and foreign interactions through the public-private partnership model.
2. **The Council Board:** After the draft agreement or policy is prepared by the Research Officers' Committee, it is forwarded to the Council Board for approval. The Council Board will consist of ministries, such as the MEA, Ministry of Finance, Ministry of Urban Development, Ministry of Climate Change, Ministry of Home Affairs, elected Mayors and Governors of respective states. This council will be headed by the chief minister of the state. The Division reviews the proposal and analyses its plausibility in foreign policy. Based on the research, the Division tries to formulate policies and draft agreements. The drafting of MoUs and the foreign policy of cities and states takes shape at this level. This division plays a crucial role in developing the diplomatic strategies of the cities and states within the framework of India's foreign policy. The Council Board will conduct meetings to evaluate the policy or agreement, which is attended by the board members and municipal corporations, if necessary. Moreover, the Board will decide on specific issues, such as how the funds

would be allocated by the central government for the project, whether the policy or agreement will have any implications for national security etc. Besides, if required, the Council Board can also suggest the Research Officers' Committee to work on specific issues, such as climate change. If needed, the draft will be sent to the Research Officers' Committee for amendments. Once the Board approves the draft, it will be subsequently sent to the Executive Committee.

3. **The Executive Committee:** The Executive Committee is the critical part of the institution as the policies and agreements are implemented by this wing. The committee will include the MEA, states' protocol officers, diplomats, states' representatives, Mayors, Governors, the MoUD and the CM. The committee will set up rules of procedure and strategies to execute the agreements and policies, such as establishing diplomatic contact with the foreign embassy, sending the itinerary to the foreign government for the foreign visits, sending the states' representatives along with the Mayor and the CM on foreign visits, assembling protocol officers, facilitating foreign dignitaries, signing of the agreement and managing relations with the sister-cities in foreign countries through follow-ups. Moreover, the executive committee has to send the progress reports to the Research Officers Committee for the annual reassessment of the policies and agreements. The committee should also report annually to the Council Board for the review of the agreements. For instance, based on the reports, the Council Board decides whether the agreement should be renewed or not.

In terms of economic activities, the SEA will closely work with the Investment Promotion Division within the MEA. Similarly, the SEA can also work in cooperation with the Indian Council for Cultural relations (ICCR) for the foreign cultural exchanges. Moreover, the allocation of funds for different projects and agreements shall be authorised by the central government. The Council Board has to provide draft policies and agreements with detailed reports on how the funds should be utilised. Furthermore, after the policy is implemented, the executive committee has to send the reports to the Comptroller and Auditor General (CAG), as mentioned under Article 148. The CAG shall audit all receipts and expenditures of the SEA. The CAG would increase the efficiency of the working of the institution by preventing corruption and other such malpractices.

The proposed model is a nascent thought. There are many questions that require extensive research, such as how to define the authority of the Parliament in the advisory board? What is the proper channel of allocation of funds from the centre to the state? How would the CAG (Comptroller and Auditor General) function under the framework of the SEA? These questions would require in-depth study, which may be undertaken in future research.

Apart from these, there are various other recommendations that could channelise the role of states in foreign policy. Happymon Jacob has suggested that state governments, with support from the MEA's States Division, can form an international cell under a senior IAS officer. Certain Indian states already have divisions dedicated to international affairs dealings in labour matters and diaspora. For instance, the Government of Kerala has a Department of Non-Resident Keralites Affairs led by a secretary-level officer. Such offices could improvise their mandate to make state governments active players in India's foreign policy making process. The newly formed Telangana is currently under the process of setting up an external affairs unit to pursue its interest and increase foreign interaction. "This new trend is indicative of an emergent recognition in state capitals that they need to do more through foreign policy to promote their interest."[20] Jacob has also suggested that the MEA should send state representatives to foreign missions. Given that the states are evolving as prominent actors of India's international relations, it is imperative that they are "encouraged and empowered to have more than occasional interactions with national, subnational and non-state actors outside."[21]

In 2020, a policy decision has been taken to launch the North Eastern Dialogue, as part of the government's paradiplomacy initiative.[22] In the case of the northeastern region, a North Eastern Council can also be developed within the Ministry of Development of North-Eastern Region (DONER). This may function under the name of 'foreign policy unit', which would focus on issues of "trade and security as well as migration and navigation."[23] However, this requires the involvement of the MEA and the central government due to security issues with China and insurgencies within the region.

Paradiplomacy in India is still in its infancy. The Modi government has placed great emphasis on cooperative federalism and city-to-city diplomacy.

Various Indian states have conducted many external activities and facilitated foreign delegations. However, the governments need a coordinated mechanism under which the states' engagements with foreign cities/provinces can be defined. The proposed model may be one such mechanism to facilitate the states' involvement in India's foreign policy. The full potential of paradiplomacy is yet to be realised in India and if it is managed early and promptly, India would emerge as a potential paradiplomatic actor and a role model at the global level. The book has made an in-depth study to uncover the journey of paradiplomacy from its interdisciplinary conception in modern diplomatic studies to its inception as a global phenomenon of the future.

Notes

1. Richard Dobbs et al., "Urban World: Mapping the Economic Power of Cities."
2. Jacob, "Putting the Periphery at the Center: Indian States' Role in Foreign Policy".
3. Narendra Modi, https://www.narendramodi.in/, https://www.narendramodi.in/text-of-prime-minister-narendra-modi-s-address-at-launch-of-multiple-development-initiatives-release-of-13th-instalment-of-pm-kisan-at-belagavi-karnataka-568194.
4. MEA, "Seventh Schedule," ed. Ministry of External Affairs, https://www.mea.gov.in/.
5. The Indian Express, "Kejriwal's Singapore Visit Canned, Govt Lashes Out," https://indianexpress.com/, https://indianexpress.com/article/cities/delhi/kejriwals-singapore-visit-canned-govt-lashes-out-8057860/.
6. "After Mea Refuses Permission for Rome Trip, Mamata Banerjee Says: Can't Stop Me Forever," https://indianexpress.com/, https://indianexpress.com/article/cities/kolkata/after-mea-refuses-permission-for-rome-trip-mamata-banerjee-says-cant-stop-me-forever-7534721/.
7. Rajib Chowdhuri, "Centre Denies Nod to Mamata for Nepal Visit," https://www.deccanchronicle.com, https://www.deccanchronicle.com/nation/politics/101221/centre-denies-didi-foreign-trip-again-west-bengal-cm-was-invited-by-n.html.
8. Jacob, "Putting the Periphery at the Center: Indian States' Role in Foreign Policy".
9. Ibid.
10. Ministry of Tourism, "Ministry of Tourism to Organise Conference on Buddhist Circuit to Promote Potential of Buddhist Tourism," https://pib.gov.in/, https://pib.gov.in/PressReleaseIframePage.aspx?PRID=1761045.

11. Ibid.
12. Tridivesh Singh Maini, "The Two Punjabs: One Step More toward Closer Cooperation?," East Asia Forum, http://www.eastasiaforum.org/2012/11/14/the-two-punjabs-one-step-more-toward-closer-cooperation/.
13. Mallica Joshi, "Pfizer, Moderna Refused to Sell Covid Vaccines Directly to Delhi, Says Arvind Kejriwal," Indian Express, https://indianexpress.com/article/cities/delhi/pfizer-moderna-refused-to-sell-covid-vaccines-directly-to-delhi-says-arvind-kejriwal-7328044/.
14. Mint, "https://www.Livemint.Com/," Mint, https://www.livemint.com/news/india/pfizer-moderna-refuse-to-send-covid-vaccines-directly-to-delhi-govt-kejriwal-11621839871304.html.
15. Marat Salikov, "The Russian Federal System: Sub-National and Local Level," Rutgers University, https://statecon.camden.rutgers.edu/sites/statecon/files/subpapers/salikov.pdf.
16. Ibid.
17. Kristyna Foltynova, "Russia Flexes Its Regional Muscle as Arctic Ice Melts," Radio Free Europe Radio Free Liberty, https://www.rferl.org/a/arctic-russia/31320776.html.
18. Ibid.
19. Alexander Sergunin & Valery Konyshev, "Forging Russia's Arctic Strategy: Actors and Decision-Making," *The Polar Journal* (2019).
20. Jacob, "Putting the Periphery at the Center: Indian States' Role in Foreign Policy".
21. Ibid.
22. MEA, "Annual Report (2020-2021)."
23. Ibid.

Bibliography

Abeywardena, Penny. "To Tackle Climate Change, We Need City Diplomacy." World Economic Forum, https://www.weforum.org/agenda/2018/05/to-tackle-climate-change-we-need-city-diplomacy-greenland-new-york/.

Agentika. "Bangalore Square," agentika.com, https://agentika.com/ru/encyclopedia/b1dc3f68-6f4e-4297-9cb9-535196800a7f/places/root/1a93d13d-01af-488d-9edc-61d76a08c2f8?version=Uwo-0.

Aguirre, Iñaki. "Making Sense of Paradiplomacy? An Intertextual Enquiry About a Concept in Search of a Definition." *Regional and Federal Studies* (2009): 185-209.

Aidarbek Amirbek, Kanat Ydyrys. "Education and Soft Power: Analysis as an Instrument of Foreign Policy." *Procedia - Social and Behavioral Sciences* 143 (2014): 514-16.

AIS. "State Protocol Officers Guidelines." All India Services: Government of India.

André Lecours, Luis Moreno. "Paradiplomacy: A Nation-Building Strategy? A Reference to the Basque Country." Chapter 12 in *The Conditions of Diversity in Multinational Democracies*, edited by Montserrat Guibernau Alain Gagnon, François Rocher, 267-92. The Institute for Research on Public Policy Canada, 2003.

Andrews, Evan. "9 Things You May Not Know About the Ancient Sumerians," www.history.com, https://www.history.com/news/9-things-you-may-not-know-about-the-ancient-sumerians.

Antonie, Ed Stoddard; Victor. "South Africa's Water Crisis Spreads from Cape Town." Reuters, https://www.reuters.com/article/us-safrica-drought-lesotho/south-africas-water-crisis-spreads-from-cape-town-idUSKBN1FK27A.

Antunes, Cátia. "Early Modern Ports, 1500–1750." EGO, http://ieg-ego.eu/en/threads/crossroads/courts-and-cities/catia-antunes-early-modern-ports-1500-1750.

ASEAN. "Asean Mekong Basin Development Cooperation", https://asean.org/, https://asean.org/asean-economic-community/asean-mekong-basin-development-cooperation-ambdc/overview/.

Atkey, Ronald G. "The Role of Provinces in International Affairs." *International Journal* 26, no. 1 (1971).

Atlas, Diercke International. "Trade and Economy in the 15th Century," http://www.diercke.com/, http://www.diercke.com/kartenansicht.xtp?artId=978-3-14-100790-9&stichwort=slave&fs=1.

Balbim, Renato. "The Workers' Party Contribution to the City Diplomacy in Brazil. A Local-Global Ideology." *Public Diplomacy of Rising and Regional Powers* 3, no. 3 (2018).

BBC. "Why Narendra Modi's First China Stop Is Xian," https://www.bbc.com/, https://www.bbc.com/news/world-asia-china-32732402.

Boyd, Eugene. "American Federalism, 1776 to 1997: Significant Events," https://usa.usembassy.de/, https://usa.usembassy.de/etexts/gov/federal.htm.

Brace, Sarah. "25 Years of Collaboration: The Pacific States/British Columbia Oil Spill Task Force 1989–2014", https://meridian.allenpress.com/.

Brasil, Governo do. "Brazil's Democratic Constitution of 1988 Was Built by Society," https://www.gov.br/pt-br, http://www.brazil.gov.br/about-brazil/news/2018/11/brazils-democratic-constitution-of-1988-was-built-by-society#:~:text=Arising%20from%20intense%20popular%20outcry,20%20months%20in%20the%20National.

bristol.gov.uk. "Twinning." Bristol City Council, https://www.bristol.gov.uk/museums-parks-sports-culture/twinning.

Britannica. "Constitutional Framework," https://www.britannica.com/, https://www.britannica.com/place/China/Constitutional-framework.

———. "Mao and the Chinese Communist Party," https://www.britannica.com/, https://www.britannica.com/biography/Mao-Zedong/Mao-and-the-Chinese-Communist-Party.

Brook, Timothy. "The Merchant Network in 16th Century China: A Discussion and Translation of Zhang Han's 'on Merchants'." *Journal of the Economic and Social History of the Orient, BRILL* 24, no. 2 (1981): 51.

brookings.edu. "México City and Chicago Announce Innovative Economic Partnership." Global Cities Initiative: Brookings, 2013.

Brown, Hannah. "Uk Cities in the Global Economy." https://www.centreforcities.org/, https://www.centreforcities.org/wp-content/uploads/2014/09/08-09-09-UK-cities-in-the-global-economy.pdf.

Buzdugan, Stephen. "New Regionalism," https://www.britannica.com/, https://www.britannica.com/topic/new-regionalism.

C40. "C40 Cities Climate Leadership Group", http://www.c40.org/.

Canada, Supreme Court of "Reference Re Secession of Quebec," https://scc-csc.lexum.com/, https://scc-csc.lexum.com/scc-csc/scc-csc/en/item/1643/index.do.

Cann, Oliver. "Time for Cities to Step up to the Challenge of Climate Change." World Economic Forum, https://www.weforum.org/press/2017/11/time-for-cities-to-step-up-to-the-challenge-of-climate-change.

Carnago, Noe. *Diplomacy and Paradiplomacy in the Redefinition of International Security: Dimensions of Conflict and Cooperation*. Paradiplomacy in Action: The Foreign Relations of Subnational Governments, edited by Michael Keating Francisco Aldecoa New York: Routledge Taylor and Francis Group, 2013.

CEMR. "Introducing Cemr." European section of United Cities and Local Governments, https://www.ccre.org/en/article/introducing_cemr.

———. "Town Twinning." European Section of United Cities and Local Governments, http://www.ccre.org/en/activites/view/9.

centerforcitizendiplomacy.org. "Sister Cities International." www.centerforcitizendiplomacy.org, https://www.centerforcitizendiplomacy.org/network/sister-cities-international/.

cgimunich.gov.in. "Indo-Baden Wurttemberg Relations." cgimunich.gov.in, https://cgimunich.gov.in/pages.php?id=12618.

cgispburg.gov.in. "India and North-West Federal Region of Russia." News release, https://cgispburg.gov.in/india-and-north-west-region-of-russian-federation.php.

———. "St. Petersburg: Fact Sheet." News release, https://cgispburg.gov.in/useful-information-about-spb.php.

CGTN. "China-Japan Ties: Ancient Temple in Japan Witnesses Centuries of Exchanges." https://news.cgtn.com/, https://news.cgtn.com/news/7a4d7a4d774d4464776c6d636a4e6e62684a4856/index.html.

Chand, Manish. "Protocol and Diplomacy: Blending Style with Substance." *In Focus* (2014). Published electronically 4th April 2014, http://www.mea.gov.in/in-focus-article.htm?23169/Protocol+and+Diplomacy+Blending+style+with+substance.

chennaimadras.blogspot.com. "Sister Act," http://chennaimadras.blogspot.com/, http://chennaimadras.blogspot.com/2008/09/sister-act.html.

China, Embassy of the People's Republic of, "Speech by Premier Wen Jiabao of the State Council of the People's Republic of China at the Japanese Diet." News release, 2007, http://lk.china-embassy.org/eng/zgxw/t311107.htm.

ChinaBriefing. "Expo Shanghai 2010," www.china-briefing.com, https://www.china-briefing.com/news/expo/.

chinacopyrightandmedia.wordpress.com. "Communiqué of the Fifth Plenary Meeting of the 18th Central Committee of the Chinese Communist Party." China Copyright and Media, https://chinacopyrightandmedia.wordpress.com/2015/10/29/communique-of-the-fifth-plenary-meeting-of-the-18th-central-committee-of-the-chinese-communist-party/.

ChinaDaily. "Shanghai Free Trade Zone Makes Impressive Progress over 7 Years." China Daily, https://www.prnewswire.com/news-releases/shanghai-free-trade-zone-makes-impressive-progress-over-7-years-301158556.html.

———. "This Day, That Year: June 24." www.chinadaily.com.cn/, https://www.chinadaily.com.cn/m/tianjinport/2019-06/24/content_37483915.htm#:~:text=On%20June%2024%2C%201973%2C%20Tianjin,for%20Friendship%20with%20Foreign%20Countries.

———. "Xi: There Is No Gene for Invasion in Our Blood." China Daily USA, http://usa.chinadaily.com.cn/china/2014-05/16/content_17511170.htm.

chinatoday.com. "The Communist Party of China (Cpc, Ccp)." China Information and Sources, http://www.chinatoday.com/org/cpc/.

Chowdhuri, Rajib. "Centre Denies Nod to Mamata for Nepal Visit," https://www.deccanchronicle.com, https://www.deccanchronicle.com/nation/politics/101221/centre-denies-didi-foreign-trip-again-west-bengal-cm-was-invited-by-n.html.

CLAIR. "Local Government International Exchange." Council of Local Authorities of International Relation, http://www.clair.or.jp/e/exchange/shimai/qanda.html.

CNM. "Quem Somos." Confederação Nacional de Municípios, https://www.cnm.org.br/institucional/conhecaacnm.

COE. "18th Plenary Session of the Congress." Council of Europe, https://rm.coe.int/168071a5b9.

councilgreatlakesregion.org. "General Info." Council of the Great Lakes Region, https://councilgreatlakesregion.org/about-cglr/.

CPAFFC. "The Chinese People's Association for Friendship with Foreign Countries (Cpaffc)." www.cpaffc.org.cn/, https://cpaffc.org.cn/index/xiehui/xiehui_list/cate/11/lang/2.html.

CSIS. "Urbanization in Sub-Saharan Africa," https://www.csis.org/, https://www.csis.org/analysis/urbanization-sub-saharan-africa.

DIPP. "Fact Sheet on Foreign Direct Investment (Fdi) from April, 2000 to June, 2017." 3, http://dipp.nic.in/sites/default/files/FDI_FactSheet_June2017_2_0.pdf: Department of Industrial Policy and Promotion, 2017.

———. "Fact Sheet on Foreign Direct Investment (Fdi) from April, 2000 to September, 2020." In *Quarterly Fact Sheet*, https://dipp.gov.in/sites/default/files/FDI_Fact_sheet_September_20.pdf: Department for Promotion of Industry and Internal Trade, 2020.

Dixit, Girish Sant and Shantanu. "The Enron Controversy: Techno-Economic Analysis and Policy Implications." Prayas: www.prayaspune.org, 1995.

Duchacek, Ivo. "The International Dimension of Subnational Self-Government." *Publius: The Journal of Federalism* (1984): 28.

ebeijing.gov.cn. "Sister Cities of Beijing," http://www.ebeijing.gov.cn/Sister_Cities_2017/.

ECLAC-UN. "Brazil - Political and Electoral System." United Nations Economic Commission for Latin America and the Caribbean, https://oig.cepal.org/en/countries/7/system.

Encyclopaedia, The Editors of. "Sumer." Britannica, https://www.britannica.com/place/Sumer.

epa.gov. "Great Lakes Restoration Initiative Action Plan Iii Fiscal Year 2020 - Fiscal Year 2024." epa.gov, epa.gov/sites/default/files/2019-10/documents/glri-action-plan-3-201910-30pp.pdf.

EU. "European Committee of the Regions (Cor)," https://european-union.europa.eu/, https://european-union.europa.eu/institutions-law-budget/institutions-and-bodies/institutions-and-bodies-profiles/cor_en.

Eurocean. "Cpmr Emphasises Need for Central Role of Regions in 'Future of Europe'," https://www.eurocean.org/, https://www.eurocean.org/np4/255.html.

EUROPA. "The Eu's Assembly of Regional and Local Representatives." European Committee of the Regions, https://cor.europa.eu/en/about/Pages/default.aspx.

Europe, Interreg. "What Is Interreg Europe?", https://www.interregeurope.eu/, https://www.interregeurope.eu/what-is-interreg-europe.

Express, The Indian. "After Mea Refuses Permission for Rome Trip, Mamata Banerjee Says: Can't Stop Me Forever," https://indianexpress.com/, https://indianexpress.com/article/cities/kolkata/after-mea-refuses-permission-for-rome-trip-mamata-banerjee-says-cant-stop-me-forever-7534721/.

———. "Kejriwal's Singapore Visit Canned, Govt Lashes Out," https://indianexpress.com/, https://indianexpress.com/article/cities/delhi/kejriwals-singapore-visit-canned-govt-lashes-out-8057860/.

facebook.com. "Embassy of India in Moscow." Official Page, https://www.facebook.com/IndiaInRussia/posts/chennai-and-volgograd-became-sister-cities-back-in-1966-they-signed-a-special-ag/3361291893913599/.

Figueiredo, Alexandre. "Paradiplomacy and National Development." VERMELHO, https://vermelho.org.br/internacional/.

Finance, California Department of. "California Becomes World's Sixth Largest Economy." World Economic Forum, 2017.

FMPRC. "Study and Implement Xi Jinping Thought on Diplomacy Conscientiously and Break New Ground in Major-Country Diplomacy with Chinese Characteristics." www.fmprc.gov.cn, https://www.fmprc.gov.cn/mfa_eng/zxxx_662805/t1799305.shtml.

FNP. "Join." Frente Nacional de Prefeitos, https://www.fnp.org.br/filie-se.

Foltynova, Kristyna. "Russia Flexes Its Regional Muscle as Arctic Ice Melts." Radio Free Europe Radio Free Liberty, https://www.rferl.org/a/arctic-russia/31320776.html.

FSI. "State Specialization by Ifs Ots of 2014 Batch." Foreign Service Institute: Government of India, 2015.

Geographic, National. "Roman Empire: Road and Trade Network." nationalgeogrophic.org, https://www.nationalgeographic.org/media/roman-empire-road-and-trade-network/.

"Global City Gdp Rankings 2008-2025." *Price Waterhouse Cooper Economic Outlook* (2009). http://pwc.blogs.com/files/global-city-gdp-rankings-2008-2025.pdf.

Goto, Junichi. "Latin Americans of Japanese Origin (Nikkeijin)", worldbank.org, https://documents1.worldbank.org/curated/en/604121468020036821/pdf/wps4203.pdf.

———. "Latin Americans of Japanese Origin (Nikkeijin) Working in Japan – a Survey", edited by World Bank Policy Research Working Paper. World Bank, 2007.

Haidar, Suhasini. "Mea to Oversee Foreign Investments in States." *The Hindu*, 2014.

Harappa.com. "Major Sites and Interaction Networks", www.harappa.com, https://www.harappa.com/indus2/161.html.

"Harmonious Urbanization: The Challenge of Balanced Territorial Development." In *The fourth session of the World Urban Forum*. Nanjing, China: UN Habitat, 2008.

Harreld, Donald J. "Merchants and International Trade Networks in the Sixteenth Century." *XIV International Economic History Congress, Helsinki* (2006): 14.

Harwit, Eric. "Taiwan's Foreign Economic Relations with Developing Nations: A Case Study of Its Ties with Palau." *The Contemporary Pacific* 12, no. 2 (2000): 465-79.

Hazarika, Obja Borah. "Evolving Dynamics of Federalism and Foreign Policy." *Indian Affairs Journal* 9, no. 1 (2014): 33-45.

ind-mum.rs.gov.ru. "Gala Concert at the Royal Opera House, Mumbai to Celebrate the 50th Anniversary of Sister Cities with St. Petersburg." News release, https://ind-mum.rs.gov.ru/en/news/21880.

india.diplo.de. "City-Friendship between Bremen and Pune." German Missions in India, https://india.diplo.de/in-de/vertretungen/gkmumbai/bremen-pune/2066692.

india.gov.in. *Constitution of India*. India: www.india.gov.in, 1950.

IULA, City Mayors: "Iula Promotes Democratic Local Governments Worldwide," http://www.citymayors.com/features/iula.html.

Jacob, Happymon. "Putting the Periphery at the Center: Indian States' Role in Foreign Policy." Carnegie India, https://carnegieindia.org/2016/10/10/putting-periphery-at-center-indian-states-role-in-foreign-policy-pub-64724.

Jain, Purnendra. *Japan's Subnational Governments in International Affairs*. 1st ed. London: Routledge, 2005. doi:https://doi.org/10.4324/9780203413906.

Jha, Prakash Chandra. "Federalism, Regionalism and States' Paradiplomacy in India." Chap. 14 In *Federalism in India: Towards a Fresh Balance of Power* edited by Lancy Lobo and Jayesh Shah, 27. Delhi: Rawat Publication, 2014.

Jianfei, Liu. "Major-Country Diplomacy with Chinese Characteristics Reflects Trends of the Times." *China International Studies* (2017), https://heinonline.org/HOL/LandingPage?handle=hein.journals/chintersd64&div=5&id=&page=.

Joshi-Ghani, Abha. "Learning to Leverage Climate Action in Cities." worldbank.org, https://blogs.worldbank.org/sustainablecities/learning-leverage-climate-action-cities.

Joshi, Mallica. "Pfizer, Moderna Refused to Sell Covid Vaccines Directly to Delhi, Says Arvind Kejriwal." Indian Express, https://indianexpress.com/article/cities/delhi/pfizer-moderna-refused-to-sell-covid-vaccines-directly-to-delhi-says-arvind-kejriwal-7328044/.

Kaj Fischer et al. "Urbanization and Climate Diplomacy." In *The Stake of Cities in Global Climate Governance*. Federal Foreign Office: Adelphi, 2015.

Kincaid, John. "Foreign Relations of Sub-National Units", https://forumfed.org/, http://www.forumfed.org/pubs/StG-Kincaid.pdf.

———. "Roles of Constituent Governments", http://www.forumfed.org/, http://www.forumfed.org/libdocs/ForRelCU01/924-FRCU0105-int-kincaid.pdf.

Konyshev, Alexander Sergunin & Valery. "Forging Russia's Arctic Strategy: Actors and Decision-Making." *The Polar Journal* (2019).

Kukucha, Chris. "Development Cooperation and Multilateralism: The Alberta Experience," http://www.forumfed.org/, http://www.forumfed.org/libdocs/2009/2008-09-18-Kukucha.pdf.

Kuznetsov, Alexander S. *Theory and Practice of Paradiplomacy*. Subnational Governments in International Affairs, edited by Markus Kornprobst Corneliu Bjola London, New York: Routledge, 2015.

Li Xiaolin, Li Xinyu. *Urban Diplomacy: Theory and Practice*. China: Social Science Academic Press, 2016.

Lisheng, Zhan. "Mayors and Urban Officials Converge in Guangzhou." China Daily, http://www.chinadaily.com.cn/cndy/2009-11/12/content_8954613.htm.

Loksabha. "Question No. 2970 New Division for Centre-State Relations," edited by Ministry of State, http://www.mea.gov.in/lok-sabha.htm?dtl/26812/QUESTION_NO2970_NEW_DIVISION_FOR_CENTRESTATE_RELATIONS: Government of India, 2016.

lomalinda-ca.gov. "Sister Cities," https://www.lomalinda-ca.gov/our_city/sister_cities.

ludwigsburg.de. "Ludwigsburg and Its Partner Cities," https://www.ludwigsburg.de/, https://www.ludwigsburg.de/site/Ludwigsburg-Internet-2020/get/params_E645929329/17943014/Ludwigsburg%20and%20its%20partner%20cities.pdf.

Maini, Tridivesh Singh. "The Two Punjabs: One Step More toward Closer Cooperation?" East Asia Forum, http://www.eastasiaforum.org/2012/11/14/the-two-punjabs-one-step-more-toward-closer-cooperation/.

Mark Amen. "Paradiplomacy in the Developing World: The Case of Brazil." Chapter 3 In *Cities and Global Governance: New Sites for International Relations*, edited by Monica Salomon. England: Ashgate Publishing Limited, 2011.

Mark, Joshua J. "Ancient Egypt." World History Encyclopedia, https://www.worldhistory.org/egypt/.

———. "Sumer." World History Encyclopedia, https://www.worldhistory.org/sumer/.

———. "Zhou Dynasty." World History Encyclopedia.

Mathew, K.S. "Calicut, the International Emporium of Maritime Trade and the Portuguese During the Sixteenth Century." *Proceedings of the Indian History Congress* 67 (2006): 19.

mcli.co.za. "Maputo Development Corridor," http://www.mcli.co.za/maputo-development-corridor/.

MEA. "Address to the Nation by Prime Minister Dr. Manmohan Singh from the Ramparts of the Red Fort, New Delhi on the 58th Independence Day." news release, 2004, https://www.mea.gov.in/Speeches-Statements.htm?dtl/3414/address+to+the+nation+by+prime+minister+dr+manmohan+singh+from+the+ramparts+of+the+red+fort+new+delhi+on+the+58th+independence+day.

———. "Annual Report (2015-2016)," edited by Ministry of External Affairs, 181-85, https://www.mea.gov.in/Uploads/PublicationDocs/26525_26525_External_Affairs_English_AR_2015-16_Final_compressed.pdf:http://www.mea.gov.in/, 2016.

———. "Annual Report (2016-2017)," edited by Ministry of External Affairs, http://www.mea.gov.in/Uploads/PublicationDocs/29521_MEA_ANNUAL_REPORT_2016_17_new.pdf:http://www.mea.gov.in/, 2017.

———. "Annual Report (2017-2018)," edited by Ministry of External Affairs, http://www.mea.gov.in/Uploads/PublicationDocs/29788_MEA-AR-2017-18-03-02-2018.pdf:http://www.mea.gov.in/, 2018.

———. "Annual Report (2018-2019)," edited by Ministry of External Affairs, http://www.mea.gov.in/Uploads/PublicationDocs/31719_MEA_AR18_19.pdf:www.mea.gov.in, 2019.

———. "Annual Report (2019-2020)," edited by Ministry of External Affairs, http://www.mea.gov.in/Uploads/PublicationDocs/32489_AR_Spread_2020_new.pdf:www.mea.gov.in, 2019.

———. "Annual Report (2020-2021)," edited by Ministry of External Affairs, http://www.mea.gov.in/Uploads/PublicationDocs/33569_MEA_annual_Report.pdf:http://www.mea.gov.in/, 2021.

———. "Annual Report (2021-2022)," edited by Ministry of External Affairs, http://www.mea.gov.in/Uploads/PublicationDocs/34894_MEA_Annual_Report_2021-22.pdf:http://www.mea.gov.in/, 2022.

———. "Annual Report (2022-2023)," edited by Ministry of External Affairs, https://mea.gov.in/Uploads/PublicationDocs/36286_MEA_Annual_Report_2022_English_web.pdf, http://www.mea.gov.in/, 2022.

———. "German Companies Are Welcome." News release, 2015, https://www.mea.gov.in/articles-in-foreign-media.htm?dtl/25060/german+companies+are+welcome.

———. "India-Japan Joint Statement During the Visit of Prime Minister to Japan." news release, 2016, https://www.mea.gov.in/bilateral-documents.htm?dtl/27599/IndiaJapan_Joint_Statement_during_the_visit_of_Prime_Minister_to_Japan.

———. "List of Commercial Documents Signed by Various Russian and Indian Entities on the Sidelines of the Prime Minister's Visit to Vladivostok," news release, 2019, https://www.mea.gov.in/bilateral-documents.htm?dtl/31801/List_of_Commercial_Documents_signed_by_various_Russian_and_Indian_entities_on_the_sidelines_of_the_Prime_Ministers_visit_to_Vladivostok.

———. "Make in India Week Curtain Raiser," news release, 2016, https://www.mea.gov.in/press-releases.htm?dtl/26334/make+in+india+week+curtain+raiser.

———. "Memorandum of Understanding between the Ministry of External Affairs, Republic of India and Chinese People's Association for Friendship with Foreign Countries on Establishment of States/Provincial Leaders' Forum," http://www.mea.gov.in/Portal/LegalTreatiesDoc/CH15B2275.pdf, 2015.

———. "Memorandum of Understanding on Cooperation between the Ministry of External Affairs of the Republic of India and the International Department of the Central Committee of the Communist Party of China," http://www.mea.gov.in/Portal/LegalTreatiesDoc/CH15B2083.pdf: Government of India, 2015.

———. "Prime Minister's Interview to the Time Magazine," News release, 2015, https://www.mea.gov.in/interviews.htm?dtl/25211/prime+ministers+interview+to+the+time+magazine.

———. "Prime Minister's Address at the Opening Ceremony of Hannover Messe." News release, 2015, https://www.mea.gov.in/Speeches-Statements.htm?dtl/25059/prime+ministers+address+at+the+opening+ceremony+of+hannover+messe+april+12+2015.

———. "Seventh Schedule," edited by Ministry of External Affairs, https://www.mea.gov.in/.

———. "Speech by Minister of State for External Affairs at the Gateway of India Dialogue (June 14)." News release, 2016, http://mea.gov.in/Speeches-Statements,htm?dtl/26910/Speech_by_Minister_of_State_for_External_Affairs_at_the_Gateway_of_India_Dialogue_June_14_2016.

———. "V. K. Singh on Q No. 687 Separate Division for Centre-State Relations," edited by Ministry of State: Government of India, 2014.

Mercociudades. "Ciudades Miembros," https://mercociudades.org/.

METI. "Memorandum of Cooperation between the Ministry of Economy, Trade and Industry (Meti) of Japan and the State Government of Gujarat of India on "Japan and India Special Program for Make in India" in Mandal-Becharaji-Khoraj, Gujarat", edited by Trade and Industry Ministry of Economy, http://www.meti.go.jp/press/2017/09/20170915006/20170915006-3.pdf: Japan, 2017.

MHA. "International Conference on Cooperative Federalism: National Perspectives and International Experience." Ministry of Home Affairs, Government of India, http://interstatecouncil.nic.in/international-conference-on-cooperative-federalism-national-perspectives-and-international-experience/.

Mierzejewski, Dominik. "Channelling Foreign Policy through Local Activities in China: City of Guangzhou - Case Study." Chap. 3 In *Paradiplomacy in Asia: Case Studies of China, India and Russia*, 94-132. Poland: Lodz University Press, 2018.

Milani, Carlos R. S. "International Relations and the Paradiplomacy of Brazilian Cities: Crafting the Concept of Local International Management." *Brazilian Administration Review* (2011).

minskherald.com. "Bangalore's Tales of Minsk Square." The Minsk Herald, http://minskherald.com/2016/01/bangalores-tales-of-minsk-square/.

Mint, "https://www.livemint.com/." Mint, https://www.livemint.com/news/india/pfizer-moderna-refuse-to-send-covid-vaccines-directly-to-delhi-govt-kejriwal-11621839871304.html.

Modi, Narendra. https://www.narendramodi.in/, https://www.narendramodi.in/text-of-prime-minister-narendra-modi-s-address-at-launch-of-multiple-development-initiatives-release-of-13th-instalment-of-pm-kisan-at-belagavi-karnataka-568194.

MOFA. "Joint Communique of the Government of Japan and the Government of the People's Republic of China," edited by Ministry of Foreign Affairs of Japan. Japan: MOFA, 1972.

MoUD. "Guidelines for Twinning of Cities," edited by Ministry of Urban Development, http://moud.gov.in/upload/uploadfiles/files/Final%20revised%20twinning%20guidelines04.pdf: Government of India, 2014.

mrif.gouv.qc.ca. "Ministère Des Relations Internationales Et De La Francophonie." Government of Québec, http://www.mrif.gouv.qc.ca/en/Ententes-et-Engagements/Ententes-internationales.

Muggah, Robert. "Cities Are on the Front-Line of Climate Change. They Must Adapt or Die." World Economic Forum, https://www.weforum.org/agenda/2016/10/cities-are-on-the-front-line-of-climate-change-they-must-adapt-or-die/.

———. "How Cities, Not States, Can Solve the World's Biggest Problems." World Economic Forum, https://www.weforum.org/agenda/2018/10/how-cities-not-states-can-solve-the-world-s-biggest-problems/.

mundalization.ca. "Twinning," https://www.mundialization.ca/activities/twinning/.

Napolitano, Marcos. "The Brazilian Military Regime, 1964-1985." *Latin American History* (2018), https://oxfordre.com/latinamericanhistory/view/10.1093/acrefore/9780199366439.001.0001/acrefore-9780199366439-e-413.

NDRC. "Vision and Actions on Jointly Building Silk Road Economic Belt and 21st-Century Maritime Silk Road." News release, 2015, https://en.ndrc.gov.cn/newsrelease_8232/201503/t20150330_1193900.html.

Nijman, Janne E. "Renaissance of the City as Global Actor. The Role of Foreign Policy and International Law Practices in the Construction of Cities as Global Actors." *T.M.C. Asser Institute for International & European Law* 2 (2016): 35.

Noah Toly, Sam Tabory. "100 Top Economies: Urban Influence and the Position of Cities in an Evolving World Order." In *Global Cities*. US: Chicago Council on Global Affairs, 2016.

Notícias, Agência Câmara de. "Pec Allows State and Municipality to Make External Agreement." News release, 2005, https://www.camara.leg.br/noticias/78558-pec-permite-a-estado-e-municipio-fazerem-acordo-externo/.

NYC.gov. "Economic Development." Mayor's Office for International Affairs, https://www1.nyc.gov/site/international/services/international-business.page.

Observatorio. "Programme Urb-Al Iii," https://www.observ-ocd.org/en/programme-urb-al-iii.

officialgazette.gov.ph. "Speech of President Arroyo During the 3rd Philippine International Sisterhood and Twinning Association, Inc. (PhISTA) Region Iv-a (Calabarzon) Chapter Assembly Cum Seminar Workshop and 1st Tourism Summit." Official Gazette, https://www.officialgazette.gov.ph/2009/10/22/speech-of-president-arroyo-during-the-3rd-philippine-international-sisterhood-and-twinning-association-inc-phista-region-iv-a-calabarzon-chapter-assembly-cum-seminar-workshop-and-1st-tourism-sum/.

Olympic.org. "Beijing 2008," https://www.olympic.org/beijing-2008.

Örtengren, Mr. "Development of Town Twinning since 1989," https://ec.europa.eu/, https://ec.europa.eu/citizenship/pdf/doc374_en.pdf.

ORU-FOGAR. "The Role of Cross-Border Cooperation." ORU-FOGAR, http://www.regionsunies-fogar.org/en/join-oru/opinion-articles/109-the-role-of-cross-border-cooperation.

Perry, Mark J. "Putting America's Ridiculously Large $18t Economy into Perspective by Comparing Us State Gdps to Entire Countries." American Enterprise Institute, https://www.aei.org/publication/putting-americas-ridiculously-large-18t-economy-into-perspective-by-comparing-us-state-gdps-to-entire-countries/.

Peter Bursens, Jana Deforche. "Going Beyond Paradiplomacy? Adding Historical Institutionalism to Account for Regional Foreign Policy Competences." *The Hague Journal of Diplomacy* 5 (2010): 151-71.

Pigeon, Mathieu. "The Quiet Revolution." McCord Museum, http://collections.musee-mccord.qc.ca/scripts/explore.php?Lang=1&elementid=109__true&tableid=11&tablename=theme&contentlong.

Pitts, Elizabeth K. "Chinese Foreign Relations in a Local Setting: The Sister City Program of the People's Republic of China." The Hong Kong University of Science and Technology, 1996.

Richard Bulliet, Pamela Crossley, Daniel Headrick, Steven Hirsch, Lyman Johnson. *The Earth and Its Peoples: A Global History*. Peoples and Civilizations of the Americas, 200-1500. Boston: Houghton Mifflin, 2008.

Richard Dobbs et al. "Urban World: Mapping the Economic Power of Cities." Mckinsey Global Institute, 2011.

Salikov, Marat. "The Russian Federal System: Sub-National and Local Level." Rutgers University, https://statecon.camden.rutgers.edu/sites/statecon/files/subpapers/salikov.pdf.

sanjosepunesistercity.org. "Stimulate Interaction between People of San Jose (Us) and Pune (India)."

Santos, Boaventura de Sousa. "Participatory Budgeting in Porto Alegre: Toward a Redistributive Democracy." *Politics & Society* 26, no. 4 (1998): 461-510, https://www.ssc.wisc.edu/~wright/santosweb.html.

seisakukikaku.metro.tokyo.lg.jp. "Tokyo's City Diplomacy." Tokyo Metropolitan Government, https://www.seisakukikaku.metro.tokyo.lg.jp/en/diplomacy/city-to-city-diplomacy/agreement.html.

Shang, Huping. *The Belth and Road Initiative: Key Concepts*. Peking University Press: Springer, 2019.

Short, John Rennie. "How Cities Are Adapting to Climate Change." World Economic Forum, https://www.weforum.org/agenda/2015/07/how-cities-are-adapting-to-climate-change/.

Shrestha, Gianna Gayle Herrera Amul and Maxim. "Cities and Climate Diplomacy in Asia Pacific." *Climate Diplomacy* (2015). www.climate-diplomacy.org

Sister-Cities, Toledo. "Toledo, Spain," http://www.toledosistercities.org/, http://www.toledosistercities.org/sistercities/toledo-spain/.

sistercities.org. "About Sister Cities International." Sister Cities International, https://sistercities.org/about-us/.

———. "Mission and History," http://www.sistercities.org/mission-and-history.

sistercitiesofla.org. "Our Sister Cities," https://sistercitiesofla.org/sister-cities/mumbai/.

Storper, Michael. "Cities and Region in the Twenty-First Century: Why Do They Develop and Change." Chap. 1 In *Keys to the City: How Economics, Institution,*

Social Interactions and Politics Shape the Development, 11. New Jersey: Princeton University Press, 2013.

Syed, Akbaruddin. "Transcript of Media Briefing by Official Spokesperson (March 7)," http://www.mea.gov.in/media-briefings.htm?dtl/23044/transcript+of+media+briefing+by+official+spokesperson+march+07+2014: Government of India, 2014.

TATNEWS.org. "Tourism Authority of Thailand and Expedia Group Announce a Memorandum of Understanding." News release, 2018, https://www.tatnews.org/2018/09/tourism-authority-of-thailand-and-expedia-group-announce-a-memorandum-of-understanding/.

Tavares, Rodrigo. "Forget the Nation-State: Cities Will Transform the Way We Conduct Foreign Affairs." World Economic Forum, https://www.weforum.org/agenda/2016/10/forget-the-nation-state-cities-will-transform-the-way-we-conduct-foreign-affairs/.

———. *Paradiplomacy: Cities and States as Global Players*. New York: Oxford University Press, 2016.

Tourism, Ministry of. "Ministry of Tourism to Organise Conference on Buddhist Circuit to Promote Potential of Buddhist Tourism," https://pib.gov.in/, https://pib.gov.in/PressReleaseIframePage.aspx?PRID=1761045.

Trone, J. *Federal Constitutions and International Relations*. University of Queensland Press, 2001.

UCLG-ASPAC. "21st Century Maritime Cooperation Committee," https://uclg-aspac.org/, https://uclg-aspac.org/en/the-21st-century-maritime-cooperation-committee/.

UN. "As World Leaders Come Together for Historic Climate Summit, Secretary-General Urges Commitment to Meaningful, Universal Agreement." News release, 2014, https://www.un.org/press/en/2014/envdev1457.doc.htm.

———. "City Summit." Paper presented at the United Nations Conference on Human Settlements (Habitat II), Istanbul, 1996.

———. "Report of the United Nations Conference on Human Settlements (Habitat II)," https://www.un.org/, https://www.un.org/ruleoflaw/wp-content/uploads/2015/10/istanbul-declaration.pdf.

———. "Report on the Ocean Conference," https://www.un.org/, https://www.un.org/sustainabledevelopment/wp-content/uploads/2017/05/Ocean-fact-sheet-package.pdf.

———. "The United Nations Advisory Committee of Local Authorities (Unacla)," https://mirror.unhabitat.org/, https://mirror.unhabitat.org/content.asp?cid=89&catid=366&typeid=24&subMenuId=0.

———. "World Entering 'Urban Millennium', Secretary-General Tells Opening Meeting of Habitat Special Session." News release, 2001, https://www.un.org/press/en/2001/GA9867.doc.htm.

UNESCWA. "International Union of Local Authorities," https://archive.unescwa.org/, https://archive.unescwa.org/international-union-local-authorities.

URB-AL. "Poverty as a Violation of Human Rights." Paper presented at the International Conference Network 10—Fight Against Urban Poverty, São Paulo, 2004.

Varghese, Peter. "Multilateral Challenges in a Federal Context." Australian Government Department of Foreign Affairs and Trade, https://www.dfat.gov.au/news/speeches/Pages/140711_fernberg.

Vargo, Jason. "Metro Sapiens: An Urban Species." *Journal of Environmental Studies and Sciences volume* 4 (17 October 2014): 360-63.

Verma, Sanjay Kumar. "Revision of Sops with Respect to Mous/Agreements with Foreign Countries," http://www.mea.gov.in/images/SOP-forwarding-letter-to-Ministries-with-revised-SOPs.pdf: Government of India, 2017.

Wendt, Alexander. "Collective Identity Information and the International State." *American Political Science Review* 88, no. 2 (1994): 384-96.

Wheare, Kenneth C. "India's New Constitution Analyzed." *The Allahabad Law Journal* 48, no. 6 (1950).

White, Matthew. "The Rise of Cities in the 18th Century," https://www.bl.uk/georgian-britain/articles/the-rise-of-cities-in-the-18th-century.

WIPO. "Constituição Da República Federativa Do Brasil De 1988 Incluindo Reformas De 1992, 1993, 1994, 1995, 1996." (2008), https://www.wipo.int/edocs/lexdocs/laws/en/br/br117en.pdf.

worldbank.org. "Cities and Climate Change: An Urgent Agenda." In *Urban Development Series Knowledge Papers*. Washington D.C: The International Bank for Reconstruction and Development/The World Bank, 2010.

www.denvergov.org. "Denver Sister Cities International", Human Rights and Community Partnerships, https://www.denvergov.org/content/denvergov/en/human-rights-and-community-partnerships/programs---initiatives/denver-sister-cities.html.

www.gov.cn. "Constitution of the People's Republic of China." The People's Republic of China, http://english.www.gov.cn/archive/lawsregulations/201911/20/content_WS5ed8856ec6d0b3f0e9499913.html.

www.grpg.org. "Sister City Seating Areas," https://www.grpg.org/, https://www.grpg.org/sister-city-seating-areas/#:~:text=Pun%C3%A9%2C%20India&text=San%20Jose%20and%20Pune%20established,on%20a%20cultural%20partnership%20since.

www.highland.gov.uk. "The City of Inverness Town Twinning Committee", The Highland Council, https://web.archive.org/web/20101231083242/http://www.highland.gov.uk/NR/rdonlyres/1C07A195-EF04-454D-81B8-ADAEE15058FC/0/ICC9908.pdf.

www.honolulu.gov. “International/Sister Cities.” City and County of Honolulu, https://www.honolulu.gov/ecodev/intl-relations/194-site-may-oed-cat/28493-city-of-mumbai.html.

Xinhuanet.com. “Pan-Beibu Gulf Economic Cooperation Forum to Be Held in October,”http://www.xinhuanet.com/,http://www.xinhuanet.com/english/2020-09/16/c_139372899.htm.

———. “The Report Analyzes China's “Urban Diplomacy”: Shifting from Focusing on Gain to Actively Giving.” China News Network, http://www.xinhuanet.com/politics/2016-03/17/c_128808031.htm.

Yanqi, Wang. “Chinese City Diplomacy Should Integrate Resources to Serve the Country's Overall Interest.” Shanghai Forum, https://shanghaiforum.fudan.edu.cn/_upload/article/files/72/67/b1c5c95043e8b02f0a89eb395770/9deb0f48-9f7c-4f89-9601-0106eb3cebf7.pdf.

Index